JOHN C. FARRELL

THE OFFICIAL

NASCAR®

TRIVIA BOOK

FENN
M&S

NASCAR® and NASCAR® Library Collection are registered trademarks of the National Association for Stock Car Auto Racing, Inc.

Library and Archives Canada Cataloguing in Publication

Farrell, John C.
Official Nascar trivia book / John C. Farrell.

ISBN 978-0-7710-5112-8

1. NASCAR (Association. – Miscellanea. 2. Stock car racing – United States – Miscellanea. I. Title.

GV1029.9S74F38 2012   796.720973   C2012-900980-6

Published simultaneously in the United States of America by Fenn/McClelland & Stewart, a division of Random House of Canada Limited Ltd., P.O. Box 1030, Plattsburgh, New York 12901

Library of Congress Control Number: 2012932380

Typeset in Scala by M&S, Toronto
Printed and bound in the United States of America

Fenn/McClelland & Stewart, a division of Random House of Canada Limited
One Toronto Street
Suite 300
Toronto, Ontario
M5C 2V6
www.mcclelland.com

1   2   3   4   5   16   15   14   13   12

For my beautiful wife, Renee,
and my two wonderful boys, Hayden and Liam.

CONTENTS

INTRODUCTION

By Marty Smith

NASCAR fans are a unique breed, among the most loyal in sport. They have an insatiable desire to learn every morsel of information possible about their chosen drivers, teams and tracks that compose the sport they love.

Whether it's Davey Allison's birth date (February 25, 1961) or how many races Dale Earnhardt won from the pole (five) or in what lap Kurt Busch's tire fell off during the 2004 finale (lap 93), we want it all.

Why? Because we love to boast this knowledge to our buddies at the break-room watercooler on Monday morning and at the neighborhood watering hole on Friday night. It's just how we're made.

That's why this book caught my eye.

Author John Farrell spent months researching and collecting data, then following up with the subjects involved to ensure accuracy of facts, figures and intricacies – and there were plenty to follow up on. In all, *The Official NASCAR Trivia Book* includes 181 little-known NASCAR details, as well as 820 trivia questions.

Farrell hoped to create a piece that included a wide range of information, from the simplest to the most obscure and difficult, so that any group of people, regardless their respective level of fandom, could participate. He succeeded.

To achieve his goal, Farrell consulted NASCAR media guides and the sport's historical database, but also leaned heavily on NASCAR's official historian, Buz McKim, and Ken Martin, from NASCAR Media Group, for guidance and interesting anecdotes from inside the garage and dusty days gone by.

I've been in the industry nearly half my life, and I learned a ton perusing this book. For example, I learned that Tim Richmond's No. 2 Buick featured a mock sponsorship from Clyde Torkle's Chicken Pit Special in the 1982 World 600 at Charlotte Motor Speedway, to promote the movie *Stroker Ace*.

And I learned that on February 9, 1952, Al Stevens caried a two-way radio in his car during the NASCAR Modified Sportsman event at Daytona Beach & Road Course, the first time two-way radio communication was used in the sport.

I also learned that Joe Frasson was fined $100 by NASCAR for beating his car with a jack handle. He was frustrated with his Pontiac after he failed to qualify for the 1975 World 600 in Charlotte, North Carolina. He later qualified for the race in Henley Gray's No. 19 Chevrolet, finishing 28th. I'll be honest: I didn't even know there was a driver named Joe Frasson.

You get the idea.

This book will educate you about NASCAR racing.

Now if you'll excuse me, I think I'll head to the watering hole and tell my buddies about Jack-Handle Joe Frasson.

MULTIPLE CHOICE

1. In which year was the first Daytona 500 held?

    a. 1948
    b. 1959
    c. 1947
    d. 1958

2. Who was the recipient of the inaugural Rookie of the Year Award in the NASCAR premier series?

    a. **Dale Earnhardt**
    b. **Shorty Rollins**
    c. **Richard Petty**
    d. **Blackie Pitt**

3. Who is the only driver to have won the NASCAR premier series championship under both the Chase for the NASCAR Sprint Cup format and the previous format?

    a. **Tony Stewart**
    b. **Jimmie Johnson**
    c. **Kurt Busch**
    d. **Jeff Gordon**

4. Who has the most career wins in the NASCAR Sprint Cup Series among active drivers as of the start of the 2012 season?

    a. Jimmie Johnson
    b. Jeff Gordon
    c. Kyle Busch
    d. Carl Edwards

5. Who is the oldest driver to have won a race in the NASCAR Nationwide Series?

    a. Harry Gant
    b. Mark Martin
    c. Jack Ingram
    d. Dick Trickle

6. Which is the only track to have consistently hosted NASCAR premier series races since the organization's inaugural year in 1949?

    a. Daytona International Speedway
    b. Watkins Glen International
    c. Martinsville Speedway
    d. Charlotte Motor Speedway

7. Which state is Greg Biffle from?

    a. **South Carolina**
    b. **California**
    c. **Washington**
    d. **New York**

8. Which TV network does not air any of NASCAR Sprint Cup Series' points races live?

    a. **ESPN**
    b. **SPEED**
    c. **ABC**
    d. **FOX**

9. Which country outside of North America hosted a NASCAR demonstration race in 1996?

    a. **Japan**
    b. **Brazil**
    c. **England**
    d. **Italy**

10. Which was the last year NASCAR allowed convertibles to compete in the NASCAR premier series?

    a. 1958
    b. 1962
    c. 1977
    d. 1984

11. Which is the current degree of banking on the corners at Dover International Speedway?

    a. **9 degrees**
    b. **18 degrees**
    c. **24 degrees**
    d. **29 degrees**

12. Which former NASCAR premier series champion only made 15 career starts in the series?

    a. **Shorty Rollins**
    b. **Rex White**
    c. **Fred Lorenzen**
    d. **Red Byron**

13. Which was the first road course to host a NASCAR premier series event?

    a. **Linden Airport**
    b. **Watkins Glen International**
    c. **Riverside International Raceway**
    d. **Bridgehampton Race Circuit**

14. In the NASCAR premier series, which driver holds the record for the most consecutive races in which they held the lead for at least one lap?

    a. **Darrell Waltrip**
    b. **Cale Yarborough**
    c. **Bobby Allison**
    d. **Richard Petty**

15. Who was not a member of the NASCAR Hall of Fame's inaugural class?

    a. **Bill France Jr.**
    b. **Bill France Sr.**
    c. **Junior Johnson**
    d. **David Pearson**

16. As of the beginning of the 2012 season, which female driver had made the most starts in the NASCAR Sprint Cup Series?

    a. **FiFi Scott**
    b. **Janet Guthrie**
    c. **Ethel Mobley**
    d. **Louise Smith**

17. Which is the term for the excess rubber build-up that is often found on the upper part of race tracks?

    a. **Marbles**
    b. **Debris**
    c. **Tire Trash**
    d. **Pebbles**

18. Which NASCAR-sanctioned track opened a 25-acre Solar Farm facility on their grounds in 2010?

    a. **Auto Club Speedway**
    b. **Daytona International Speedway**
    c. **Pocono Raceway**
    d. **Watkins Glen International**

19. Which driver won the first-ever sanctioned NASCAR Camping World Truck Series race, which was held at Phoenix International Raceway on February 5, 1995?

    a. **Ron Hornaday Jr.**
    b. **Johnny Benson**
    c. **Mike Skinner**
    d. **Terry Labonte**

20. Which driver has won the most races in a single Chase for the NASCAR Sprint Cup?

    a. **Jimmie Johnson**
    b. **Tony Stewart**
    c. **Kyle Busch**
    d. **Carl Edwards**

21. As of the beginning of the 2012 season, which driver in the NASCAR premier series has won the most pole awards on road courses during their career?

    a. **Terry Labonte**
    b. **Jeff Gordon**
    c. **David Pearson**
    d. **Darrell Waltrip**

22. The Titusville-Cocoa Speedway in Titusville, Florida, has hosted only one race in the NASCAR premier series. The race was held on December 30, 1956. Who was the winner?

    a. **Lee Petty**
    b. **Glenn "Fireball" Roberts**
    c. **Paul Goldsmith**
    d. **Joe Weatherly**

23. At which track did Richard Petty earn his first victory in the NASCAR premier series?

    a. **Martinsville Speedway**
    b. **Darlington Raceway**
    c. **Southern States Fairgrounds**
    d. **Occoneechee Speedway**

24. Which NASCAR premier series driver won the first NASCAR Most Popular Driver Award?

    a. **Bill Elliott**
    b. **Lee Petty**
    c. **Fred Lorenzen**
    d. **Curtis Turner**

25. Which driver has the most career NASCAR Most Popular Driver Awards in the NASCAR premier series?

    a. **Richard Petty**
    b. **Bill Elliott**
    c. **Dale Earnhardt Jr.**
    d. **Bobby Allison**

26. Which track's nickname is "The Beast of the Southeast"?

    a. **Atlanta Motor Speedway**
    b. **Charlotte Motor Speedway**
    c. **Daytona International Speedway**
    d. **Talladega Superspeedway**

27. Tar Heel Speedway was located in which North Carolina city?

    a. **Chapel Hill**
    b. **Concord**
    c. **Randleman**
    d. **Tarboro**

28. When was ground broken for the construction of the NASCAR Hall of Fame in Charlotte, North Carolina?

    a. **May 11, 2007**
    b. **June 19, 2007**
    c. **December 17, 2006**
    d. **January 25, 2007**

29. Which is the only race car number to be retired in a NASCAR series?

    a. **No. 3**
    b. **No. 43**
    c. **No. 61**
    d. **No. 76**

30. Who drove the car that had its number retired per the previous question?

    a. **Dale Earnhardt**
    b. **Richie Evans**
    c. **Richard Petty**
    d. **Glenn "Fireball" Roberts**

31. Which driver was nicknamed "The Silver Fox"?

    a. **David Pearson**
    b. **Ronnie Silver**
    c. **Bobby Allison**
    d. **Paul Goldsmith**

32. Which current NASCAR Sprint Cup Series driver won twice at Pocono Raceway during his rookie season?

    a. **Jimmie Johnson**
    b. **Bobby Labonte**
    c. **Denny Hamlin**
    d. **Greg Biffle**

33. Which driver took 544 starts to record his 10th win in the NASCAR premier series?

    a. **Harry Gant**
    b. **Kasey Kahne**
    c. **Geoff Bodine**
    d. **Sterling Marlin**

34. Which of the following drivers did not win at least one race every year between 2002 and 2011 in the NASCAR Sprint Cup Series?

    a. Jimmie Johnson
    b. Tony Stewart
    c. Matt Kenseth
    d. Kurt Busch

35. Going into the 2012 season, which NASCAR Sprint Cup Series driver has the most victories in the series at Texas Motor Speedway?

    a. Jeff Burton
    b. Denny Hamlin
    c. Matt Kenseth
    d. Carl Edwards

36. Which track was added to the NASCAR Sprint Cup Series schedule for the first time in 2011?

    a. Chicagoland Speedway
    b. Kentucky Speedway
    c. Las Vegas Motor Speedway
    d. Nashville Superspeedway

37. Which is the maximum number of points a driver can earn in a NASCAR Sprint Cup Series race?

a. 43
b. 195
c. 48
d. 185

38. Which NASCAR Sprint Cup Series driver has the longest active streak of seasons with at least one pole award?

a. Jeff Gordon
b. Ryan Newman
c. Mark Martin
d. Kyle Busch

39. Which NASCAR Sprint Cup Series track was the sport's first paved superspeedway?

a. Daytona International Speedway
b. Martinsville Speedway
c. Richmond International Raceway
d. Darlington Raceway

40. Who was the first race car driver to post a speed faster than 200 mph in a stock car?

    a. **Richard Petty**
    b. **Bill Elliott**
    c. **Buddy Baker**
    d. **David Pearson**

41. Which moment in the early 1970s is considered by most to be the beginning of what is called the "modern era" of the NASCAR premier series?

    a. **R.J. Reynolds bringing their Winston brand to NASCAR as a title sponsor**
    b. **Trimming the schedule from 48 races to 31**
    c. **Bill France Sr. handing over the reins of the sport to his son, Bill France Jr.**
    d. **The final dirt-track race of the NASCAR premier series**

42. Which is the average weight of a NASCAR Sprint Cup Series race car without the driver?

    a. **3,125 pounds**
    b. **3,450 pounds**
    c. **3,575 pounds**
    d. **3,700 pounds**

43. Which brother of a current NASCAR Sprint Cup Series driver won the 2010 NASCAR K&N Pro Series East championship?

    a. **Brian Keselowski**
    b. **Kerry Earnhardt**
    c. **Ryan Truex**
    d. **Jarit Johnson**

44. Which is the term for the upper area of a race car that extends from the base of the windshield in the front, the tops of doors on the sides and the base of the rear window in the back?

    a. **Chassis**
    b. **Bell Housing**
    c. **Setup**
    d. **Greenhouse**

45. Which NASCAR Sprint Cup Series driver's pit crew won the NASCAR Sprint Pit Crew Challenge in 2009?

    a. **Jeff Burton**
    b. **Jeff Gordon**
    c. **Denny Hamlin**
    d. **Juan Pablo Montoya**

46. Which of the following states has never hosted a NASCAR Sprint Cup Series race?

    a. **South Dakota**
    b. **Louisiana**
    c. **Utah**
    d. **Maine**

47. Which of the following states has hosted a NASCAR Sprint Cup Series race?

    a. **Idaho**
    b. **Oklahoma**
    c. **Mississippi**
    d. **Vermont**

48. Which NASCAR executive was featured going undercover as Kevin Thomas in an episode of CBS's hit show *Undercover Boss*?

    a. **Mike Helton**
    b. **Brian France Jr.**
    c. **Steve Phelps**
    d. **Robin Pemberton**

49. Which term do race teams usually use to refer to new race car tires?

    a. **Newbies**
    b. **Slicks**
    c. **Stickers**
    d. **Grippers**

50. Which of the following sports did Jimmie Johnson participate in at his high school?

    a. **Football**
    b. **Soccer**
    c. **Basketball**
    d. **Water Polo**

51. Which over-the-wall pit-crew position did NASCAR eliminate in 2011?

    a. **Catch Can Man**
    b. **Windshield Cleaner**
    c. **Jackman**
    d. **Front Grille Engineer**

52. Which is the term for the part of the tire that touches the surface of the track?

   a. **Sweet Spot**
   b. **Contact Patch**
   c. **Touch Point**
   d. **Impact Rubber**

53. What did Dale Earnhardt Jr. want to be if he hadn't become a race car driver?

   a. **Zookeeper**
   b. **Sportscaster**
   c. **Veterinarian**
   d. **Mechanic**

54. In terms of miles run, which track hosts the shortest NASCAR Sprint Cup Series race?

   a. **Bristol Motor Speedway**
   b. **Sonoma**
   c. **Richmond International Raceway**
   d. **Martinsville Speedway**

55. How many gallons of fuel can the average fuel cell on a NASCAR Sprint Cup Series race car hold?

   a. 18 gallons
   b. 17 gallons
   c. 19 gallons
   d. 17.5 gallons

56. Which current NASCAR Sprint Cup Series driver's foundation published the popular book *Pit Road Pets* and its sequel *Pit Road Pets: The Second Lap*?

   a. Greg Biffle
   b. Jeff Burton
   c. Dale Earnhardt Jr.
   d. Ryan Newman

57. Which of the following drivers was not involved in the famous brawl that occurred at the end of the 1979 Daytona 500?

   a. Bobby Allison
   b. Donnie Allison
   c. Richard Petty
   d. Cale Yarborough

58. Of the four races considered to be the crown jewels on the 1985 NASCAR premier series schedule, which one did Bill Elliott not win?

a. **Daytona 500**
b. **Winston 500**
c. **Coca-Cola 600**
d. **Southern 500**

59. At which race track did Dale Earnhardt win his final NASCAR premier series race?

a. **Atlanta Motor Speedway**
b. **Charlotte Motor Speedway**
c. **Daytona International Speedway**
d. **Talladega Superspeedway**

60. Other than Jimmie Johnson, who is the only driver to win three consecutive championships in the NASCAR premier series?

a. **Richard Petty**
b. **Cale Yarborough**
c. **Darrell Waltrip**
d. **Dale Earnhardt**

61. Which current owner is often referred to as "The Cat in the Hat"?

a. **Richard Childress**
b. **Joe Gibbs**
c. **Rick Hendrick**
d. **Jack Roush**

62. Which NASCAR premier series driver has the most second-place finishes throughout his career?

a. **Richard Petty**
b. **David Pearson**
c. **Bobby Allison**
d. **Dale Earnhardt**

63. At which track did 1950 NASCAR premier series champion Bill Rexford earn his only pole in the series?

a. **Daytona Beach & Road Course**
b. **North Wilkesboro Speedway**
c. **Canfield Fairgrounds**
d. **Morristown Speedway**

64. Which track has the nickname "The Great American Speedway"?

    a. **Daytona International Speedway**
    b. **Texas Motor Speedway**
    c. **Charlotte Motor Speedway**
    d. **Chicagoland Speedway**

65. The late Vice President of Corporate Communications and Weekly Touring Series for NASCAR, Jim Hunter, wrote several books on racing, but only one that was on a specific driver. Who was that driver?

    a. **Cale Yarborough**
    b. **Richard Petty**
    c. **David Pearson**
    d. **Bobby Allison**

66. Of the following, which is not a nickname for NASCAR premier series driver Fred Lorenzen?

    a. **Big Race Fred**
    b. **Golden Boy**
    c. **Fearless Freddie**
    d. **Elmhurst Express**

67. Which NASCAR premier series driver's car helped inspire the character Doc Hudson in the movie *Cars*?

    a. **Marshall Teague**
    b. **Dick Rathmann**
    c. **Tim Flock**
    d. **Lee Petty**

68. Which NASCAR premier series driver raced with a special brace on his left leg to accommodate a World War II injury?

    a. **Bud Moore**
    b. **Fonty Flock**
    c. **Buck Baker**
    d. **Red Byron**

69. Which NASCAR premier series driver did *Sports Illustrated* tab as the "Babe Ruth of Stock Car Racing"?

    a. **Cale Yarborough**
    b. **Curtis Turner**
    c. **Lee Petty**
    d. **Ned Jarrett**

70. Which former NASCAR Sprint Cup Series driver, along with his wife and Paul Newman, fulfilled his late son's dreams by building Victory Junction in Randleman, North Carolina, which is a camp for children with chronic medical conditions and serious illnesses?

a. **Kyle Petty**
b. **Jimmie Johnson**
c. **Ryan Newman**
d. **Jeff Gordon**

71. Wendell Scott is the first African-American driver to win a race in the NASCAR premier series. At which track did he capture this victory?

a. **Piedmont Interstate Fairgrounds**
b. **Dog Track Speedway**
c. **Speedway Park**
d. **Birmingham International Raceway**

72. Who is the only NASCAR Sprint Cup Series driver to win three consecutive poles at Sonoma?

a. **Jeff Gordon**
b. **Kasey Kahne**
c. **Ernie Irvan**
d. **Ricky Rudd**

73. Which of the following drivers was not part of "The Alabama Gang"?

    a. **Red Byron of Anniston, Alabama**
    b. **Neil Bonnett of Bessemer, Alabama**
    c. **Donnie Allison of Hueytown, Alabama**
    d. **Red Farmer of Hialeah, Florida**

74. Before Ricky Rudd broke the record for most consecutive starts in the NASCAR premier series in 2002, who held the streak?

    a. **Terry Labonte**
    b. **Rusty Wallace**
    c. **Jeff Gordon**
    d. **Richard Petty**

75. At which track was the first NASCAR premier series race west of the Mississippi River held?

    a. **Tucson Rodeo Grounds**
    b. **Carrell Speedway**
    c. **Marchbanks Speedway**
    d. **Lincoln City Fairgrounds**

76. Which driver won the final race at the famed Daytona Beach & Road Course?

    a. **Lee Petty**
    b. **Rex White**
    c. **Curtis Turner**
    d. **Paul Goldsmith**

77. Which NASCAR premier series driver was the first to rack up double-digit wins in a single season?

    a. **Herb Thomas**
    b. **Speedy Thompson**
    c. **Dick Rathmann**
    d. **Buck Baker**

78. Which driver won the first Winston-sponsored race in the NASCAR premier series?

    a. **Bobby Allison**
    b. **Jim Vandiver**
    c. **Donnie Allison**
    d. **Dave Marcis**

79. Who was the first African-American driver to compete in a NASCAR premier series event?

    a. **Wendell Scott**
    b. **Charlie Scott**
    c. **Eliso Bowie**
    d. **Willy T. Ribbs**

80. Who was the first Hispanic-American driver to compete in a NASCAR premier series race?

    a. **Frank Mundy**
    b. **Jimmy Florian**
    c. **Lou Figaro**
    d. **Frank Oviado**

81. Which NASCAR premier series driver scored Ford's first victory in the series?

    a. **Speedy Thompson**
    b. **Ned Jarrett**
    c. **Jimmy Florian**
    d. **Buck Baker**

82. Three female race car drivers participated in the July 4, 1977, race at Daytona International Speedway. Who did not appear in the race?

    a. Janet Guthrie
    b. Lella Lombardi
    c. Christine Beckers
    d. Robin McCall

83. Which driver holds the distinction of being the first to be black-flagged during a NASCAR race?

    a. Junior Johnson
    b. Richard Petty
    c. Herman Beam
    d. Bobby Johns

84. Who drove the first convertible to compete in any NASCAR series race?

    a. Don Oldenberg
    b. Jim Paschal
    c. Tim Flock
    d. Herk Moak

85. Which caused the January 23, 1972, race at Riverside International Raceway in California to be stopped 42 laps prematurely?

    a. **Track falling apart**
    b. **Blizzard**
    c. **Heavy fog**
    d. **Strike**

86. At which track did the NASCAR premier series hold its 1,000th race, which was run in 1971?

    a. **Ontario Motor Speedway**
    b. **Daytona International Speedway**
    c. **Greenville-Pickens Speedway**
    d. **Smokey Mountain Raceway**

87. At which track did the NASCAR premier series hold its 2,000th race, which was run in 2003?

    a. **Texas Motor Speedway**
    b. **Darlington Raceway**
    c. **Atlanta Motor Speedway**
    d. **Bristol Motor Speedway**

88. Who was the first driver in the NASCAR premier series to start in the last position of the starting grid and go on to win the race?

    a. **Marvin Panch**
    b. **Jim Cook**
    c. **Dick Rathmann**
    d. **Bill Amick**

89. Which was Dale Earnhardt's first name?

    a. **Dale**
    b. **Randy**
    c. **Ralph**
    d. **William**

90. In which sport did Glenn "Fireball" Roberts earn his nickname?

    a. **NASCAR**
    b. **Baseball**
    c. **Track**
    d. **Football**

91. Who is considered NASCAR's first officially licensed artist?

    a. **Sam Bass**
    b. **Garry Hill**
    c. **Thomas Kinkade**
    d. **Charles Fazzino**

92. Which NASCAR premier series star declined Mickey Thompson's invitation to drive Thompson's car in the 1962 Indianapolis 500?

    a. **Junior Johnson**
    b. **Richard Petty**
    c. **Glenn "Fireball" Roberts**
    d. **David Pearson**

93. Which was the original acronym that was accepted by the group that met in a hotel in Daytona Beach, Florida, to discuss forming a sanctioning body for stock car racing in 1947?

    a. **NSCRA**
    b. **SCARA**
    c. **SCRA**
    d. **NARSC**

94. Which member in attendance at the initial meetings to discuss NASCAR's formation suggested the National Association for Stock Car Auto Racing (NASCAR) as an option?

    a. **Frank Mundy**
    b. **Bill France**
    c. **Raymond Parks**
    d. **Red Vogt**

95. Which feature made the Langhorne Speedway unique?

    a. **There was a lake in the infield**
    b. **It was circular**
    c. **It was on an old army base**
    d. **All of the above**

96. Which is former NASCAR premier series driver Coo Coo Marlin's real first name?

    a. **Clifton**
    b. **Coo Coo**
    c. **James**
    d. **Sterling**

97. For which NASCAR owner did Tony Stewart win his first two NASCAR Sprint Cup Series championships?

    a. **Rick Hendrick**
    b. **Jack Roush**
    c. **Gene Haas**
    d. **Joe Gibbs**

98. Which number race car did Dale Earnhardt drive in his NASCAR premier series debut at Charlotte Motor Speedway on May 25, 1975?

    a. **No. 2**
    b. **No. 8**
    c. **No. 30**
    d. **No. 77**

99. Which was Dale Earnhardt's car sponsor in his NASCAR premier series debut at Charlotte Motor Speedway on May 25, 1975?

    a. **Army Special**
    b. **Hy Gain**
    c. **10,000 RPM**
    d. **Belden Asphalt**

100. Which denomination of U.S. currency are some NASCAR drivers superstitious about touching?

    a. **$1 bill**
    b. **$5 bill**
    c. **$20 bill**
    d. **$50 bill**

101. Which was the only year Richard Petty drove Fords in the NASCAR premier series?

    a. **1969**
    b. **1973**
    c. **1979**
    d. **1981**

102. Name the former NASCAR driver who is now the pace car driver for NASCAR Sprint Cup Series events.

    a. **Neil Bonnett**
    b. **Ricky Rudd**
    c. **Brett Bodine**
    d. **Ernie Irvan**

103. Who was the first NASCAR premier series driver to win a race behind the steering wheel of the No. 3 race car?

    a. **Dick Rathmann**
    b. **Paul Goldsmith**
    c. **Dale Earnhardt**
    d. **Glenn "Fireball" Roberts**

104. As of the beginning of the 2012 season, which of the following race cars has only three total victories in the NASCAR premier series?

    a. **No. 22**
    b. **No. 19**
    c. **No. 82**
    d. **No. 62**

105. Who was the first driver to pilot a Rick Hendrick–owned race car in the NASCAR premier series?

    a. **Tim Richmond**
    b. **Dick Brooks**
    c. **Geoff Bodine**
    d. **Jeff Gordon**

106. Who won the inaugural NASCAR Sprint Cup Series race at Chicagoland Speedway in 2001?

    a. Tony Stewart
    b. Kevin Harvick
    c. Todd Bodine
    d. Ryan Newman

107. Which NASCAR executive became the organization's third president in 2000?

    a. Bill France Jr.
    b. Brian France
    c. Robin Pemberton
    d. Mike Helton

108. Which company sponsored Dale Earnhardt Jr.'s race car in his second and third career starts in the NASCAR Nationwide Series at Nashville Speedway and Watkins Glen International in 1997?

    a. Wrangler
    b. Church Brothers
    c. Gargoyles
    d. AC Delco

109. Who won the only NASCAR premier series race at Pine Grove Speedway, which took place on October 14, 1951?

    a. **Billy Carden**
    b. **Tim Flock**
    c. **Hap Jones**
    d. **Wimpy Ervin**

110. The inaugural NASCAR premier series race, the 1960 World 600, at Charlotte Motor Speedway was won by which driver?

    a. **Joe Lee Johnson**
    b. **Tiny Lund**
    c. **David Pearson**
    d. **Herman Beam**

111. Which was the nickname of Jeff Gordon's colorful DuPont-sponsored crew from the 1990s?

    a. **The Color Brigade**
    b. **The Crayon Crew**
    c. **The Young Guns**
    d. **The Rainbow Warriors**

112. Which driver won the pole award for the inaugural NASCAR premier series race at Indianapolis Motor Speedway in 1994 and then only led for the first two laps of the race before finishing 22nd?

    a. **Wally Dallenbach Jr.**
    b. **Rick Mast**
    c. **Geoff Bodine**
    d. **Jimmy Spencer**

113. Who won the inaugural NASCAR premier series race at Indianapolis Motor Speedway in 1994, leading 93 of the 160 laps?

    a. **Bill Elliott**
    b. **Jeff Gordon**
    c. **Dale Earnhardt**
    d. **Terry Labonte**

114. Which former NFL star co-owned a NASCAR Camping World Truck Series team from July 2008 through the 2011 season and had Jimmie Johnson, Mike Skinner, Travis Kvapil, Landon Cassill, Tyler Malsam and Todd Bodine, among others, pilot his trucks?

    a. **Troy Aikman**
    b. **Julius Peppers**
    c. **Roger Staubach**
    d. **Randy Moss**

115. Which slang term is used for a series of acute left- and right-hand turns on a road course where the turns immediately follow one another?

 a. **Esses**
 b. **Snakes**
 c. **Zags**
 d. **Cutbacks**

116. Who was NASCAR's first championship-winning owner in the NASCAR premier series in 1949?

 a. **Glen Wood**
 b. **Bud Moore**
 c. **Raymond Parks**
 d. **Glenn Dunaway**

117. How many races did Ned Jarrett compete in during his last season, the 49-race season of 1966, which was the year after he won his second NASCAR premier series championship?

 a. **3**
 b. **21**
 c. **38**
 d. **49**

118. Which current NASCAR Sprint Cup Series driver won the 2007 championship in what is now the NASCAR K&N Pro Series East?

    a. **Michael McDowell**
    b. **Joey Logano**
    c. **Landon Cassill**
    d. **Brad Keselowski**

119. At which track did Dale Earnhardt Jr. earn his first victory in the NASCAR premier series?

    a. **Rockingham Speedway**
    b. **Pocono Raceway**
    c. **Texas Motor Speedway**
    d. **Talladega Superspeedway**

120. Which classic movie was featured on the paint schemes of Jeff Gordon's, Elliott Sadler's, Brendan Gaughan's and Scott Riggs' race cars for the October 10, 2004, NASCAR premier series race?

    a. *Star Wars*
    b. *Gone with the Wind*
    c. *E.T.*
    d. *The Wizard of Oz*

121. Which artist designed the bright paint scheme for the No. 3 Chevrolet that Dale Earnhardt drove in the 2000 NASCAR All-Star Race?

    a. **Sam Bass**
    b. **Peter Max**
    c. **Thomas Kinkade**
    d. **Andy Warhol**

122. At which track did what is now known as the NASCAR Nationwide Series make its Mexican debut in 2005?

    a. **Autodromo Hermanos Rodriguez**
    b. **Autodromo Potosino**
    c. **Nuevo Autodromo de Queretaro**
    d. **Nuevo Autodromo de Aguascalientes**

123. How many races did Dale Earnhardt and Dale Inman work together as driver and crew chief in the 1981 NASCAR premier series season before Earnhardt left to drive for Jim Stacy?

    a. **1**
    b. **11**
    c. **16**
    d. **20**

124. Which NASCAR premier series driver won his first race in the series at Savannah Speedway (Georgia) on May 1, 1964?

    a. Jimmy Pardue
    b. LeeRoy Yarbrough
    c. Curtis Crider
    d. Cale Yarborough

125. How many drivers lined up for the start of the inaugural Southern 500 at Darlington Raceway (South Carolina) on September 4, 1950?

    a. 22
    b. 36
    c. 55
    d. 75

126. Which of the following was not a sponsor of any of the Flock brothers during the 1951 NASCAR premier series season?

    a. Black Phantom
    b. Blue Banshee
    c. Gray Ghost
    d. Red Devil

127. Who won the only NASCAR premier series race run at Gastonia Fairgrounds (North Carolina), which was held on September 12, 1958, after leading only the final lap?

    a. **Bob Welborn**
    b. **Lee Petty**
    c. **Buck Baker**
    d. **Shorty Rollins**

128. Which of the following race car numbers did Bobby Allison not win a NASCAR premier series race while driving?

    a. **No. 11**
    b. **No. 14**
    c. **No. 16**
    d. **No. 29**

129. In which year was Atlanta Motor Speedway's configuration reversed?

    a. **1993**
    b. **1995**
    c. **1997**
    d. **1999**

130. Which driver gave Richard Childress Racing its first NASCAR premier series victory?

    a. **Dale Earnhardt**
    b. **Ricky Rudd**
    c. **Richard Childress**
    d. **Kirk Shelmerdine**

131. As of the start of the 2012 season, which NASCAR Sprint Cup Series driver has the most victories in the series at Chicagoland Speedway in Joliet, Illinois?

    a. **Tony Stewart**
    b. **Kevin Harvick**
    c. **Jeff Gordon**
    d. **Kyle Busch**

132. Which of the following car makes joined GRAND-AM Road Racing as an Official Promotional Partner in early February 2012?

    a. **Ferrari**
    b. **Ford**
    c. **Porsche**
    d. **Nissan**

133. Which company sponsored the race car Matt Kenseth drove to a sixth-place finish in his first NASCAR premier series start, which was at Dover International Speedway, on September 20, 1998?

    a. **McDonald's**
    b. **DeWalt**
    c. **Lycos**
    d. **Kraft**

134. In 1958, which driver was voted by Florida's sportswriters as the Professional Athlete of the Year?

    a. **Lee Petty**
    b. **Junior Johnson**
    c. **Glenn "Fireball" Roberts**
    d. **Speedy Thompson**

135. In 2010, which NASCAR executive did H.A. Branham write a NASCAR-licensed book about?

    a. **Bill France Sr.**
    b. **Bill France Jr.**
    c. **Mike Helton**
    d. **Brian France**

136. Who won the first NASCAR premier series race on June 19, 1949, held at Charlotte Speedway in North Carolina?

    a. Jim Roper
    b. Bob Flock
    c. Curtis Turner
    d. Jack Smith

137. Who was named the first commissioner of NASCAR in 1948?

    a. Raymond Parks
    b. Red Byron
    c. Bill France Sr.
    d. Erwin "Cannonball" Baker

138. Who won the final NASCAR premier series race at the popular Rockingham Speedway in North Carolina?

    a. Bill Elliott
    b. Dale Jarrett
    c. Matt Kenseth
    d. Jeff Burton

139. Who won the inaugural NASCAR premier series race at Las Vegas Motor Speedway on March 1, 1998?

    a. Jeff Gordon
    b. Dale Jarrett
    c. Bobby Labonte
    d. Mark Martin

140. Who was the first female driver to appear in a NASCAR premier series race?

    a. Sara Christian
    b. Louise Smith
    c. Janet Guthrie
    d. Ethel Flock

141. Which former NASCAR premier series champion quit school as a teenager to work at a sawmill?

    a. Buck Baker
    b. Bobby Isaac
    c. Bill Rexford
    d. Joe Weatherly

142. Who sat atop the No. 17 DeWalt war wagon as Matt Kenseth's crew chief for the 2008 NASCAR Sprint Cup season?

a. **Chip Bolin**
b. **Drew Blickensderfer**
c. **Robbie Reiser**
d. **Bob Osborne**

143. Which 2011 Chase for the NASCAR Sprint Cup contender exhibited his breakdancing skills in Las Vegas during the 2011 Champion's Week?

a. **Denny Hamlin**
b. **Carl Edwards**
c. **Jeff Gordon**
d. **Tony Stewart**

144. Richard Petty won seven NASCAR premier series champion-ships during his storied career. He primarily drove a Plymouth during four of those championship seasons and a Dodge during two. However, in 1979, his final championship season, which make did Petty enter most races driving?

a. **Ford**
b. **Buick**
c. **Mercury**
d. **Chevrolet**

145. Which current NASCAR driver appeared on an episode of the History Channel's *American Pickers*, when the two hosts picked something they felt this driver would be interested in buying?

    a. Jimmie Johnson
    b. Ryan Newman
    c. Austin Dillon
    d. Mark Martin

146. Which NASCAR track has a lake named "Lake Lloyd" in its infield?

    a. Daytona International Speedway
    b. Talladega Superspeedway
    c. Indianapolis Motor Speedway
    d. Michigan International Speedway

147. Which Cartoon Network show did Carl Edwards appear on?

    a. *Phineas and Ferb*
    b. *Rated A for Awesome*
    c. *Kick Buttowski: Suburban Daredevil*
    d. *Pair of Kings*

148. Which country is NASCAR Sprint Cup Series driver Marcos Ambrose from?

    a. **Brazil**
    b. **Canada**
    c. **Australia**
    d. **South Africa**

149. Which year did Bristol Motor Speedway host its first NASCAR premier series race?

    a. **1961**
    b. **1959**
    c. **1981**
    d. **1973**

150. Which current NASCAR Sprint Cup Series driver hosted *Saturday Night Live* on January 11, 2003?

    a. **Jeff Gordon**
    b. **Tony Stewart**
    c. **Dale Earnhardt Jr.**
    d. **Matt Kenseth**

151. Of which college basketball team is Virginia native Jeff Burton a huge fan?

    a. **Virginia Tech Hokies**
    b. **North Carolina Tarheels**
    c. **Virginia Cavaliers**
    d. **Duke Blue Devils**

152. In the 10 years that the Daytona Beach & Road Course was on the NASCAR premier series schedule, two drivers won two series events at the track, more than any other driver. Who were they?

    a. **Red Byron and Harold Kite**
    b. **Marshall Teague and Tim Flock**
    c. **Lee Petty and Bill Blair**
    d. **Cotton Owens and Paul Goldsmith**

153. Which track gives a Ridgeway grandfather clock to the winners of its NASCAR Sprint Cup Series events as a trophy?

    a. **Richmond International Raceway**
    b. **Sonoma**
    c. **Watkins Glen International**
    d. **Martinsville Speedway**

154. In 1997, Robby Gordon earned his one and only pole award (as of the beginning of the 2012 season) at which track?

   a. **Atlanta Motor Speedway**
   b. **Daytona International Speedway**
   c. **Darlington Raceway**
   d. **New Hampshire Motor Speedway**

155. Which is the name of Dover International Speedway's mascot?

   a. **Goliath**
   b. **Miles**
   c. **Lightning**
   d. **Dover**

156. In 2008, Carl Edwards finished second in the NASCAR Sprint Cup Series final points standings behind champion Jimmie Johnson. However, Edwards finished with the most victories in the series that season. How many trips to Victory Lane did Edwards take in the series that year?

   a. **7**
   b. **8**
   c. **9**
   d. **10**

157. Which of the following drivers did not appear in a 2011 episode of A&E's *The Glades*?

    a. Joey Logano
    b. Tony Stewart
    c. Jeff Gordon
    d. Brian Vickers

158. Which cable network premiered the NASCAR news/talk show *Inside NASCAR* prior to the beginning of the 2010 season?

    a. ESPN
    b. HBO
    c. SHOWTIME
    d. SPEED

159. Which former NASCAR driver joined the cast of *Inside NASCAR* prior to the 2011 season?

    a. Dale Jarrett
    b. Kyle Petty
    c. Bill Elliott
    d. Ricky Rudd

160. Which track currently hosting NASCAR Sprint Cup Series events has the largest seating capacity?

    a. **Daytona International Speedway**
    b. **Indianapolis Motor Speedway**
    c. **Bristol Motor Speedway**
    d. **Las Vegas Motor Speedway**

161. When Dale Earnhardt made his famous "pass in the grass" in 1987, which driver did he supposedly overtake?

    a. **Terry Labonte**
    b. **Ricky Rudd**
    c. **Tim Richmond**
    d. **Bill Elliott**

162. In which 1987 race did Dale Earnhardt make his "pass in the grass"?

    a. **Daytona 500**
    b. **Southern 500**
    c. **NASCAR Sprint All-Star Race**
    d. **Coca-Cola 600**

163. In 2013, Victory Junction is scheduled to open its second camp for children with chronic medical conditions and serious illnesses. In which state will the new facility be built?

    a. **Florida**
    b. **California**
    c. **New Hampshire**
    d. **Kansas**

164. As of the beginning of the 2012 season, other than Kentucky Speedway (which was added to the NASCAR Sprint Cup Series schedule beginning in 2011), which is the only current track where Jeff Gordon has not won a NASCAR Sprint Cup event?

    a. **Texas Motor Speedway**
    b. **Homestead-Miami Speedway**
    c. **Phoenix International Raceway**
    d. **Las Vegas Motor Speedway**

165. On January 16, 2012, it was announced that David Ragan would drive the No. 34 race car full-time in the upcoming NASCAR Sprint Cup Series season for which team?

    a. **Front Row Motorsports**
    b. **Roush Fenway Racing**
    c. **Richard Petty Motorsports**
    d. **Michael Waltrip Racing**

166. How many victories in the NASCAR premier series did David Pearson have while driving for Wood Brothers between 1972 and 1978 and only running partial schedules?

    a. 21
    b. 35
    c. 43
    d. 52

167. For the October 2011 Talladega race, NASCAR increased the size of the holes in the restrictor plate. Which was the size of the holes in the restrictor plates used in the race?

    a. 1-inch diameter
    b. 61/64-inch diameter
    c. 57/64-inch diameter
    d. 52/64-inch diameter

168. Which of the following political figureheads visited Homestead-Miami Speedway for the 2011 Ford Championship Weekend?

    a. Michelle Obama
    b. Newt Gingrich
    c. Bill Clinton
    d. Joe Biden

169. Which country music superstar hosted the 2011 NASCAR Sprint Cup Series Awards Ceremony?

    a. Blake Shelton
    b. Trace Adkins
    c. Willie Nelson
    d. Reba McEntire

170. After leaving Penske Racing following the 2011 season, which racing team did Kurt Busch sign on to drive with in 2012?

    a. Furniture Row Racing
    b. Phoenix Racing
    c. Tommy Baldwin Racing
    d. Germain Racing

171. Which state did Jeff Gordon grow up in?

    a. California
    b. New York
    c. Indiana
    d. North Carolina

172. Which is Ryan Newman's nickname?

    a. **Rocket Man**
    b. **The Engineer**
    c. **Lightning**
    d. **Professor**

173. In which year did Rick Hendrick first enter a race car in NASCAR premier series competition?

    a. **1980**
    b. **1982**
    c. **1984**
    d. **1986**

174. At which NASCAR premier series track did Cale Yarborough win his first race in the series?

    a. **Old Dominion Speedway**
    b. **Valdosta 75 Speedway**
    c. **Beltsville Speedway**
    d. **Rockingham Speedway**

175. Trenton Speedway in New Jersey is which unconventional track shape?

    a. **Figure eight**
    b. **Hexagon**
    c. **Kidney**
    d. **Light bulb**

176. Which movie star was the Grand Marshal for the 1962 Southern 500 at Darlington Raceway?

    a. **Gregory Peck**
    b. **Peter O'Toole**
    c. **Sean Connery**
    d. **Clint Eastwood**

177. Eutechnyx, the developer of the video game *NASCAR: The Game 2011*, has its headquarters located where?

    a. **Newcastle, Washington**
    b. **Newcastle, England**
    c. **Newcastle, Oklahoma**
    d. **Newcastle, Australia**

178. On July 18, 1958, Canadian National Exhibition Speedway in Toronto hosted its only NASCAR premier series race. Which driver won the 100-lap event?

   a. **Lee Petty**
   b. **Cotton Owens**
   c. **Rex White**
   d. **Shorty Rollins**

179. Who won the only NASCAR premier series event to be held at Stamford Park in Niagara Falls, Ontario, which took place on July 1, 1952?

   a. **Herb Thomas**
   b. **Buddy Shuman**
   c. **Fonty Flock**
   d. **Albert Lemieux**

180. Who won the Chisholm Speedway (Montgomery, Alabama) NASCAR premier series event on September 9, 1956, the only time the series raced at the track?

   a. **Marvin Panch**
   b. **Lee Petty**
   c. **Tim Flock**
   d. **Buck Baker**

181. Who won the only NASCAR premier series event ever held at Dixie Speedway in Birmingham, Alabama, which took place on August 3, 1960?

    a. **Maurice Petty**
    b. **Ned Jarrett**
    c. **Richard Petty**
    d. **Neil Castles**

182. On August 8, 1962, Huntsville Speedway (Alabama) hosted its only NASCAR premier series race. Which driver won the 200-lap event, leading all 200 laps?

    a. **Joe Weatherly**
    b. **Ned Jarrett**
    c. **Richard Petty**
    d. **Bob Welborn**

183. Who won the only NASCAR premier series event ever held at Tucson Rodeo Grounds (Arizona), which took place on May 15, 1955?

    a. **Danny Letner**
    b. **Bill Amick**
    c. **Ray Clark**
    d. **Lloyd Dane**

184. Who won the Capitol Speedway (Sacramento, California) NASCAR premier series event on June 22, 1957, the only time the series raced at the track?

    a. **Bill Amick**
    b. **Lloyd Dane**
    c. **Parnelli Jones**
    d. **Art Watts**

185. On June 3, 1956, Merced Fairgrounds in California hosted its only NASCAR premier series race. Which driver won the 200-lap race?

    a. **Herb Thomas**
    b. **Eddie Pagan**
    c. **Sherman Clark**
    d. **Lucky Long**

186. Who won the only NASCAR premier series event ever held at Santa Clara Fairgrounds (California), which took place on September 15, 1957?

    a. **Jim Hurtubise**
    b. **Jim Cook**
    c. **Lloyd Dane**
    d. **Marvin Porter**

187. Who won the only NASCAR premier series event ever held at Five Flags Speedway in Pensacola, Florida, which took place on June 14, 1953?

    a. **Dick Passwater**
    b. **Herb Thomas**
    c. **Gober Sosebee**
    d. **Jim Paschal**

188. Who won the second race of the 1963 NASCAR premier series season, which was held at Golden Gate Speedway in Tampa, Florida, the only race in the series the track has ever hosted?

    a. **Possum Jones**
    b. **Jimmie Pardue**
    c. **Richard Petty**
    d. **Joe Weatherly**

189. Who won the only NASCAR premier series event ever held at Augusta International Raceway in Georgia, which took place on November 17, 1963?

    a. **Glenn "Fireball" Roberts**
    b. **Marvin Panch**
    c. **David Pearson**
    d. **Larry Thomas**

190. The Columbus Speedway in Georgia has hosted only one race in the NASCAR premier series. It took place on June 10, 1951. Who was the winner of the race?

    a. **Donald Thomas**
    b. **Lee Petty**
    c. **Frank Mundy**
    d. **Tim Flock**

191. Who won the only NASCAR premier series event ever held at Hayloft Speedway in Augusta, Georgia, which took place on June 1, 1952?

    a. **June Cleveland**
    b. **Tommy Moon**
    c. **Bill Snowden**
    d. **Gober Sosebee**

192. Davenport Speedway in Iowa has hosted only one race in the NASCAR premier series. It was held on August 2, 1953. Who won the race?

    a. **Dick Rathmann**
    b. **Herb Thomas**
    c. **Johnny Beauchamp**
    d. **Tubby Harrison**

193. Who won the only NASCAR premier series event ever held at Funks Speedway in Winchester, Indiana, which took place on October 15, 1950?

    a. **Lloyd Moore**
    b. **Bud Boone**
    c. **Jimmy Florian**
    d. **Dick Linder**

194. Corbin Speedway (Kentucky) has hosted only one race in the NASCAR premier series. It was held on August 29, 1954. Who won the race?

    a. **Lee Petty**
    b. **Hershel McGriff**
    c. **Joe Eubanks**
    d. **John Smith**

195. Who won the only NASCAR premier series race ever held at Louisiana Fairgrounds in Shreveport, which took place on June 7, 1953?

    a. **Tim Flock**
    b. **Gober Sosebee**
    c. **Lee Petty**
    d. **Slick Smith**

196. Norwood Arena hosted its only NASCAR premier series race on June 17, 1961, with Emanuel Zervakis winning the 125-mile event. In which state is the quarter-mile track found?

a. **Massachusetts**
b. **North Carolina**
c. **Oklahoma**
d. **Washington**

197. Tim Flock won the only NASCAR premier series race to be held at Monroe Speedway (Michigan), which took place on July 6, 1952. Which make of race car did Flock drive to victory at the half-mile track?

a. **Oldsmobile**
b. **Plymouth**
c. **Packard**
d. **Hudson**

198. Who won the only NASCAR premier series race ever held at Harnett Speedway in Spring Lake, North Carolina, which took place on March 8, 1953?

a. **Dick Rathmann**
b. **Herb Thomas**
c. **Mike Klapak**
d. **Lee Petty**

199. Who won the 29th race of the 1958 NASCAR premier season, which was held at McCormick Field in Asheville, North Carolina? It was the only series event the makeshift track ever hosted.

a. **Cotton Owens**
b. **Rex White**
c. **Junior Johnson**
d. **Jim Paschal**

200. Which NASCAR premier series champion has won the Daytona 500 a record seven times?

a. **Jeff Gordon**
b. **Bobby Allison**
c. **Richard Petty**
d. **Junior Johnson**

201. Salisbury Super Speedway in North Carolina has hosted only one NASCAR premier series race. It was run on October 5, 1958. Who won the race?

a. **Lee Petty**
b. **Cotton Owens**
c. **Buck Baker**
d. **Tiny Lund**

202. Star Lite Speedway hosted only one NASCAR premier series race. It was held on May 13, 1966, with Darel Dieringer winning the 250-lap event. In which state is the half-mile track found?

   a. **California**
   b. **Florida**
   c. **North Carolina**
   d. **Wisconsin**

203. Who won the only NASCAR premier series race ever held at Lincoln City Fairgrounds in North Platte, Nebraska, which took place on July 26, 1953?

   a. **Byron Clouse**
   b. **Dick Rathmann**
   c. **Herb Thomas**
   d. **Marvin Copple**

204. Wall Stadium in Belmar, New Jersey, hosted its only NASCAR premier series race ever on July 26, 1958. Who won the race?

   a. **Jim Reed**
   b. **Buzz Woodward**
   c. **Speedy Thompson**
   d. **Rex White**

205. Who won the only NASCAR premier series race ever held at Las Vegas Park Speedway in Nevada, which took place on October 16, 1955?

    a. **Bill Hyde**
    b. **Bill West**
    c. **Bob Stanclift**
    d. **Norm Nelson**

206. Airborne Speedway hosted its only NASCAR premier series event on June 19, 1955, with Lee Petty winning while leading 163 of the 200 laps. In which state is the half-mile track found?

    a. **New Hampshire**
    b. **New Jersey**
    c. **New Mexico**
    d. **New York**

207. Buffalo Civic Stadium hosted its only NASCAR premier series event on July 19, 1958, with Jim Reed winning while leading 55 laps of the 100 laps. Which make race car did Reed pilot to victory?

    a. **Pontiac**
    b. **Ford**
    c. **Chevrolet**
    d. **Oldsmobile**

208. Who won the only NASCAR premier series race ever held at Montgomery Air Base (New York), which took place on July 17, 1960?

    a. **Richard Petty**
    b. **Lee Petty**
    c. **Rex White**
    d. **Ned Jarrett**

209. State Line Speedway, located in Busti, New York, hosted its only NASCAR premier series event on July 16, 1958. Who won the race?

    a. **Shorty Rollins**
    b. **Bob Finale**
    c. **Bill Poor**
    d. **Emory Mahon**

210. Who won the only NASCAR premier series race ever run at Kitsap County Airport in Bremerton, Washington, which took place on August 4, 1957?

    a. **Parnelli Jones**
    b. **Ed Negre**
    c. **Scotty Cain**
    d. **Lloyd Dane**

211. Wine Creek Race Track, located in Owego, New York, hosted its only NASCAR premier series event on July 4, 1952. Who won the race?

    a. **Bucky Sager**
    b. **Dick Rathmann**
    c. **Lee Petty**
    d. **Tim Flock**

212. Who won the 28th race of the 1953 NASCAR premier series season at Princess Anne Speedway in Norfolk, Virginia? Held on August 23, 1953, it was the only event in the series the track ever hosted.

    a. **Andy Winfree**
    b. **Herb Thomas**
    c. **Lee Petty**
    d. **Fonty Flock**

213. Who won the only NASCAR premier series event ever held at Powell Motor Speedway in Columbus, Ohio, which took place on May 24, 1953?

    a. **Fonty Flock**
    b. **Curtis Turner**
    c. **Herb Thomas**
    d. **Bub King**

214. Who won the only NASCAR premier series event ever held at Sharon Speedway in Hartford, Ohio, which took place on May 23, 1954?

    a. **Lee Petty**
    b. **Buck Baker**
    c. **Dick Rathmann**
    d. **Joe Eubanks**

215. Oklahoma State Fairgrounds in Oklahoma City hosted its only NASCAR premier series event on August 3, 1956, with Jim Paschal leading only 7 of the 200 laps on his way to victory. Which make race car was Paschal driving?

    a. **Ford**
    b. **Chevrolet**
    c. **Chrysler**
    d. **Mercury**

216. The 33rd race of the 1953 NASCAR premier series season was held at Bloomsburg Fairgrounds (Pennsylvania) on October 3. Who won the race?

    a. **Bob Welborn**
    b. **Ted Chamberlain**
    c. **Herb Thomas**
    d. **Wimpy Ervin**

217. Who won the only NASCAR premier series event ever held at New Bradford Speedway in Bradford, Pennsylvania, which took place on June 12, 1958?

   a. **Billy Rafter**
   b. **Junior Johnson**
   c. **Jack Smith**
   d. **Speedy Thompson**

218. On October 14, 1951, Tim Flock won the only NASCAR premier series event ever held at Pine Grove Speedway. In which state is the track found?

   a. **Maine**
   b. **Delaware**
   c. **Wisconsin**
   d. **Pennsylvania**

219. Herb Thomas won the only NASCAR premier series race ever held at Williams Grove Speedway in Mechanicsburg, Pennsylvania, on June 27, 1954. What make was the car Thomas piloted to victory?

   a. **Nash**
   b. **Studebaker**
   c. **Hudson**
   d. **Dodge**

220. Who won the only NASCAR premier series event ever held at Gamecock Speedway in Sumter, South Carolina, which took place on September 15, 1960?

    a. **Ned Jarrett**
    b. **Richard Petty**
    c. **David Pearson**
    d. **Doug Yates**

221. How many drivers entered the September 15, 1960, race at Gamecock Speedway in Sumter, South Carolina?

    a. **13**
    b. **29**
    c. **48**
    d. **71**

222. On June 23, 1971, which NASCAR premier series driver started on the pole and led 253 of the 300 laps to capture the checkered flag in the only series race ever held at Meyer Speedway in Houston, Texas?

    a. **James Hylton**
    b. **Bobby Allison**
    c. **J.D. McDuffie**
    d. **Cecil Gordon**

223. Who won the only NASCAR premier series race ever held at Newberry Speedway in South Carolina, which was run on October 12, 1957?

    a. **Brownie King**
    b. **Bill Amick**
    c. **Marvin Panch**
    d. **Glenn "Fireball" Roberts**

224. On July 22, 1953, Rapid Valley Speedway in Rapid City, South Dakota, hosted its only NASCAR premier series race. Who won?

    a. **Herb Thomas**
    b. **Johnny Beauchamp**
    c. **Lee Petty**
    d. **Fonty Flock**

225. Who won the only NASCAR premier series race ever held at Hartsville Speedway in South Carolina, which took place on June 23, 1961?

    a. **David Pearson**
    b. **Junior Johnson**
    c. **Buck Baker**
    d. **Ned Jarrett**

226. Which 2011 Chase for the NASCAR Sprint Cup contender had an average placing of 4.9 in the last 10 races of the season, the highest average finish?

    a. **Carl Edwards**
    b. **Tony Stewart**
    c. **Jimmie Johnson**
    d. **Jeff Gordon**

227. At which track did NASCAR premier series driver Jack White win his only first-place finish in the series?

    a. **Hamburg Speedway**
    b. **Daytona Beach & Road Course**
    c. **Vernon Fairgrounds**
    d. **Martinsville Speedway**

228. Who was the highest-placing female driver in the August 27, 1950, NASCAR premier series event at Hamburg Speedway in New York?

    a. **Ethel Mobley**
    b. **Ann Chester**
    c. **Sara Christian**
    d. **Louise Smith**

229. Earl Balmer appeared in 32 races between 1959 and 1968, winning only one of them. What year did he win one of the Twin 125s at Daytona International Speedway?

  a. **1959**
  b. **1964**
  c. **1966**
  d. **1967**

230. Johnny Benson won 14 races in the NASCAR Camping World Truck Series and 3 races in what is now the NASCAR Nationwide Series, but he only has one victory in the NASCAR premier series. At which track did Benson earn his 2002 victory?

  a. **Kansas Speedway**
  b. **Las Vegas Motor Speedway**
  c. **Pocono Raceway**
  d. **Rockingham Speedway**

231. In his 18 years on the NASCAR premier series, Brett Bodine had only one victory. At which track did he get his win?

  a. **Talladega Superspeedway**
  b. **North Wilkesboro Speedway**
  c. **Bristol Motor Speedway**
  d. **Dover International Speedway**

232. The now-defunct NASCAR Speedway Division ran for only two years. Buck Baker was crowned the division's champion in 1952, but which driver was crowned the champion in its second and final season?

    a. **Buck Baker**
    b. **Pete Allen**
    c. **Glen Wood**
    d. **Lee Petty**

233. On June 16, 1962, Johnny Allen of Greenville, South Carolina, earned his one and only trip to Victory Lane. At which track was he victorious?

    a. **Concord Speedway**
    b. **South Boston Speedway**
    c. **Bowman Gray Stadium**
    d. **Southside Speedway**

234. Dick Brooks of Porterville, California, won only one race in his NASCAR premier series career. At which track did he win?

    a. **Talladega Superspeedway**
    b. **Darlington Raceway**
    c. **Nashville Speedway**
    d. **Richmond International Raceway**

235. At which track did Bob Burdick of Omaha, Nebraska, win his only NASCAR premier series race?

a. **Ascot Stadium**
b. **Martinsville Speedway**
c. **Occoneechee Speedway**
d. **Atlanta Motor Speedway**

236. On October 14, 1951, Marvin Burke of Pittsburg, California, won the only race he started in the NASCAR premier series. At which track did he win?

a. **Oakland Stadium**
b. **Marchbanks Speedway**
c. **Central City Speedway**
d. **Arizona State Fairgrounds**

237. At which track did Neil Cole earn his only trip to Victory Lane as a driver in the NASCAR premier series?

a. **Dayton Speedway**
b. **Occoneechee Speedway**
c. **Thompson Speedway**
d. **Morristown Speedway**

238. California native Jim Cook won only one race in the NASCAR premier series. At which track did this victory come?

    a. **Charlotte Motor Speedway**
    b. **California State Fairgrounds**
    c. **Marchbanks Speedway**
    d. **Red Speedway**

239. Mark Donohue competed in only six races in the NASCAR premier series during his career (1972–73), winning one. At which track did he cross the finish line first?

    a. **Riverside International Raceway**
    b. **Atlanta Motor Speedway**
    c. **Ontario Motor Speedway**
    d. **Daytona International Speedway**

240. At which track did Joe Eubanks win his only NASCAR premier series race?

    a. **Darlington Raceway**
    b. **Salisbury Super Speedway**
    c. **Occoneechee Speedway**
    d. **Martinsville Speedway**

241. Lou Figaro appeared in 13 races in the 1951 NASCAR premier series season while only getting one win, which was his only career win in the series. At which track did Figaro finish first?

   a. **Carrell Speedway**
   b. **Fort Miami Speedway**
   c. **Columbia Speedway**
   d. **Canfield Fairgrounds**

242. John Soares only competed in 11 races in his NASCAR premier series career, managing just one victory. At which track did Soares win?

   a. **Oakland Stadium**
   b. **Bay Meadows Race Track**
   c. **Langhorne Speedway**
   d. **Carrell Speedway**

243. Larry Frank won only one race during his 11-year career in the NASCAR premier series (1956–66). In which year did that victory occur?

   a. **1956**
   b. **1959**
   c. **1962**
   d. **1965**

244. Danny Graves won only one race in his nine-race NASCAR premier series career. At which track did Graves visit Victory Lane?

    a. **Ascot Stadium**
    b. **Portland Speedway**
    c. **California State Fairgrounds**
    d. **Jacksonville Speedway**

245. Royce Haggerty piloted the No. 15N Dodge to his only victory in the NASCAR premier series. Where did Haggerty earn the victory?

    a. **Redwood Speedway**
    b. **Bay Meadows Race Track**
    c. **Daytona Beach & Road Course**
    d. **Portland Speedway**

246. Bobby Hillin Jr. of Midland, Texas, won only one NASCAR premier series event during his career. At which track did he win?

    a. **Talladega Superspeedway**
    b. **Watkins Glen International**
    c. **Dover International Speedway**
    d. **Charlotte Motor Speedway**

247. At which track did Jim Hurtubise get his only victory in the NASCAR premier series?

   a. **Atlanta Motor Speedway**
   b. **Bristol Motor Speedway**
   c. **Charlotte Motor Speedway**
   d. **Daytona International Speedway**

248. John Kieper won only one race in his NASCAR premier series career. At which track did he win?

   a. **Merced Fairgrounds**
   b. **Portland Speedway**
   c. **Redwood Speedway**
   d. **California State Fairgrounds**

249. At which NASCAR premier series track did Harold Kite get his only win in the series?

   a. **Darlington Raceway**
   b. **North Wilkesboro Speedway**
   c. **Columbia Speedway**
   d. **Daytona Beach & Road Course**

250. Which NASCAR Sprint Cup Series crew chief left Tony Stewart's team after winning the 2011 championship to lead Denny Hamlin's team during the 2012 season?

a. **Greg Zipadelli**
b. **Mike Ford**
c. **Darian Grubb**
d. **Steve Addington**

251. Paul Lewis earned the only NASCAR premier series victory of his career in 1966. At which track did he collect this win?

a. **Hickory Speedway**
b. **Smokey Mountain Raceway**
c. **Asheville-Weaverville Speedway**
d. **Nashville Speedway**

252. Johnny Mantz got his only NASCAR premier series victory at which track?

a. **Dayton Speedway**
b. **Darlington Raceway**
c. **Occoneechee Speedway**
d. **Michigan State Fairgrounds**

253. On July 4, 1966, Sam McQuagg led 126 of the 160 laps to win the NASCAR premier series race at Daytona International Speedway, his only victory in the series. Which was the margin of victory he had over second-place finisher Darel Dieringer?

    a. 0.05 seconds
    b. 1.8 seconds
    c. 1 minute 6 seconds
    d. 11 laps

254. At which track did Lake Speed earn his only victory in the NASCAR premier series?

    a. **Darlington Raceway**
    b. **North Wilkesboro Speedway**
    c. **Bristol Motor Speedway**
    d. **Riverside International Raceway**

255. Chuck Stevenson earned his first (and only) victory in the NASCAR premier series after competing in just two races. Which track hosted this race?

    a. **Road America**
    b. **Portland Speedway**
    c. **Willow Springs Speedway**
    d. **Hickory Speedway**

256. At which track did Jerry Nadeau earn his only victory in the NASCAR premier series?

    a. **New Hampshire Motor Speedway**
    b. **Indianapolis Motor Speedway**
    c. **Bristol Motor Speedway**
    d. **Atlanta Motor Speedway**

257. At which track did Donald Thomas score his only victory in the NASCAR premier series?

    a. **Dayton Speedway**
    b. **Occoneechee Speedway**
    c. **Lakewood Speedway**
    d. **Langhorne Speedway**

258. At which track did Bill Norton score his only victory in the NASCAR premier series?

    a. **Oakland Stadium**
    b. **Bainbridge Fairgrounds**
    c. **Marchbanks Speedway**
    d. **Carrell Speedway**

259. In 1988, Phil Parsons of Denver, North Carolina, won the only race of his NASCAR premier series career. At which track did Parsons clinch the victory?

   a. **Daytona International Speedway**
   b. **Talladega Superspeedway**
   c. **Bristol Motor Speedway**
   d. **Charlotte Motor Speedway**

260. At which track did Dick Passwater get the only victory of his 20 career starts in the NASCAR premier series?

   a. **Charlotte Speedway**
   b. **Harnett Speedway**
   c. **Powell Motor Speedway**
   d. **Louisiana Fairgrounds**

261. Lennie Pond raced in the NASCAR premier series between 1969 and 1989, winning his only race in 1978. At which track did he claim his victory?

   a. **Nashville Speedway**
   b. **Talladega Superspeedway**
   c. **Dover International Speedway**
   d. **Riverside International Raceway**

262. At which track did Tommy Thompson earn his only victory in the NASCAR premier series?

    a. **Dayton Speedway**
    b. **Darlington Raceway**
    c. **Daytona Beach & Road Course**
    d. **Michigan State Fairgrounds**

263. Bill Rexford of Conowango Valley, New York, made 36 career starts in the NASCAR premier series, scoring only one victory in his five seasons. At which track did Rexford earn the win?

    a. **Canfield Fairgrounds**
    b. **Monroe County Fairgrounds**
    c. **Vernon Fairgrounds**
    d. **Funks Speedway**

264. At which track did Jody Ridley cross the finish line first in the NASCAR premier series?

    a. **Dover International Speedway**
    b. **Texas World Speedway**
    c. **Richmond International Raceway**
    d. **Atlanta Motor Speedway**

265. Prior to the beginning of the 2012 NASCAR Sprint Cup Series, Martin Truex Jr. had claimed one victory in the series. At which track did he win?

  a. **Auto Club Speedway**
  b. **Las Vegas Motor Speedway**
  c. **Dover International Speedway**
  d. **Chicagoland Speedway**

266. On April 28, 1957, Art Watts won the NASCAR premier series event at Portland Speedway in Oregon in what would be the only series win of his career. How old was Watts at the time?

  a. **26**
  b. **37**
  c. **39**
  d. **46**

267. At which NASCAR premier series track did Earl Ross earn his only win in the series?

  a. **Pocono Raceway**
  b. **Martinsville Speedway**
  c. **Ontario Motor Speedway**
  d. **Charlotte Motor Speedway**

268. John Rostek only appeared in six races in his NASCAR premier series career, winning just once. At which track did this victory occur?

    a. **Arizona State Fairgrounds**
    b. **Marchbanks Speedway**
    c. **Martinsville Speedway**
    d. **Montgomery Air Base**

269. At which NASCAR premier series track did Greg Sacks claim his only victory in the series?

    a. **Riverside International Raceway**
    b. **Talladega Superspeedway**
    c. **Atlanta Motor Speedway**
    d. **Daytona International Speedway**

270. Ron Bouchard appeared in 22 of 31 races in the 1981 NASCAR premier series, winning once in what would be his only victory in the series. At which track did he pick up that win?

    a. **Talladega Superspeedway**
    b. **Bristol Motor Speedway**
    c. **North Wilkesboro Speedway**
    d. **Atlanta Motor Speedway**

271. Leon Sales appeared in only two races in the 1950 NASCAR premier series season (and only eight in his entire career). winning one of them. At which track did he earn his victory?

 a. Martinsville Speedway
 b. North Wilkesboro Speedway
 c. Darlington Raceway
 d. Occoneechee Speedway

272. At which track did Frankie Schneider claim his only race win in the NASCAR premier series?

 a. Starkey Speedway
 b. Old Bridge Stadium
 c. Old Dominion Speedway
 d. Champion Speedway

273. In 1951, Danny Weinberg began his seven-year NASCAR premier series career by appearing in six races and finishing first in one. At which track did he win what would turn out to be his only career victory?

 a. Carrell Speedway
 b. Arizona State Fairgrounds
 c. Marchbanks Speedway
 d. Oakland Stadium

274. Which businessman, after a trip to the Indianapolis 500, was inspired to build a speedway in Darlington, South Carolina?

    a. Jim Hunter
    b. Bill France
    c. Raymond Parks
    d. Harold Brasington

275. Who won the only Daytona 500 to start on Monday night in prime time?

    a. Richard Petty
    b. Matt Kenseth
    c. Jimmie Johnson
    d. Jeff Gordon

276. Which city has never hosted the NASCAR Sprint Cup Series Awards Ceremony?

    a. Charlotte, North Carolina
    b. Daytona Beach, Florida
    c. Las Vegas, Nevada
    d. New York, New York

277. In which year did Sunoco become the Official Fuel of NASCAR?

  a. 1993
  b. 1999
  c. 2004
  d. 2010

278. Who was the first rookie in the NASCAR premier series to win the NASCAR Sprint All-Star Race?

  a. Jimmie Johnson
  b. Dale Earnhardt Jr.
  c. Terry Labonte
  d. Davey Allison

279. As of the start of the 2012 season, which female driver has posted the highest finish in a race in any of the top-3 NASCAR national touring series?

  a. Sara Christian
  b. Shawna Robinson
  c. Danica Patrick
  d. Louise Smith

280. Which two past NASCAR premier series champions completed their championship seasons with 42 top-5 finishes?

   a. **Ned Jarrett and David Pearson**
   b. **David Pearson and Richard Petty**
   c. **Dale Earnhardt and Richard Petty**
   d. **Bobby Isaac and Cale Yarborough**

281. As of the end of the 2012 season, which car manufacturer has won the most NASCAR Manufacturers Championships?

   a. **Plymouth**
   b. **Ford**
   c. **Chevrolet**
   d. **Dodge**

282. Which Ford model was raced in the 2012 NASCAR Sprint Cup Series season?

   a. **Thunderbird**
   b. **Fusion**
   c. **Mustang**
   d. **Taurus**

283. Which actress served as the Grand Marshal for the March 10, 1963, NASCAR premier series race at Occoneechee Speedway?

    a. **Shirley McLaine**
    b. **Natalie Wood**
    c. **Patricia Neal**
    d. **Jayne Mansfield**

284. Which current NASCAR driver has a daughter who won the 2011 ASA Late Model championship at I-44 Lebanon Speedway in Missouri?

    a. **Joe Nemechek**
    b. **Mike Wallace**
    c. **Dave Blaney**
    d. **Kenny Wallace**

285. How many people attended the meetings Bill France called in late 1947 to discuss the future of stock car racing?

    a. **26**
    b. **35**
    c. **36**
    d. **40**

286. Which of the following drivers was not in attendance at the late 1947 meetings to discuss the future of stock car racing?

    a. **Lee Petty**
    b. **Sammy Packard**
    c. **Red Byron**
    d. **Fonty Flock**

287. Which stock car pioneer became the first multi-team owner in stock car racing?

    a. **Lee Petty**
    b. **Raymond Parks**
    c. **Glen Wood**
    d. **Carl Kiekhaefer**

288. Which NASCAR pioneer did Bill France Sr. award NASCAR's first membership card to?

    a. **Raymond Parks**
    b. **Bill Tuthill**
    c. **Mildred Ayres**
    d. **Red Vogt**

289. Which team owner is credited with first uniforming his pit crews?

    a. **Carl Kiekhaefer**
    b. **Glen Wood**
    c. **Harold Kite**
    d. **Bud Moore**

290. Who was the first factory-funded driver in NASCAR?

    a. **Fonty Flock**
    b. **Herb Thomas**
    c. **Marshall Teague**
    d. **Lee Petty**

291. In which year did Bill France Sr. first compete in a stock car race?

    a. **1936**
    b. **1940**
    c. **1944**
    d. **1948**

292. Which of the following years did Richard Petty not win the NASCAR premier series championship?

    a. 1964
    b. 1967
    c. 1969
    d. 1979

293. In which year did NASCAR introduce roof flaps for the race cars?

    a. 1981
    b. 1987
    c. 1991
    d. 1994

294. Which company developed Lexan?

    a. **DuPont**
    b. **Roush Industries**
    c. **BASF**
    d. **General Electric**

295. Who was the first driver to qualify a stock car at over 200 mph?

    a. **Bill Elliott**
    b. **Junior Johnson**
    c. **Benny Parsons**
    d. **Richard Petty**

296. Which of the following race car numbers did Richard Petty not win a NASCAR premier series race while driving?

    a. **No. 41**
    b. **No. 42**
    c. **No. 43**
    d. **No. 44**

297. Who is the oldest driver to win the NASCAR premier series championship?

    a. **Lee Petty**
    b. **Dale Jarrett**
    c. **Bobby Allison**
    d. **Dale Earnhardt**

298. Which was the highest position in the final points standings that Tim Richmond placed during a season in the NASCAR premier series?

    a. **Second**
    b. **Third**
    c. **Fourth**
    d. **Fifth**

299. In 1982, who won the first race at Daytona International Speedway in what is now the NASCAR Nationwide Series?

    a. **Jack Ingram**
    b. **Sam Ard**
    c. **Dale Earhnhardt**
    d. **Darrell Waltrip**

300. Which driver won 10 races during the 2008 NASCAR Nationwide Series season?

    a. **Carl Edwards**
    b. **Brad Keselowski**
    c. **Denny Hamlin**
    d. **Kyle Busch**

301. Which driver won the first NASCAR premier series race held at Pocono Raceway?

    a. **Richard Petty**
    b. **David Pearson**
    c. **Benny Parsons**
    d. **Cale Yarborough**

302. Which NASCAR premier series driver won back-to-back Coca-Cola 600s in 1982 and 1983?

    a. **Harry Gant**
    b. **Neil Bonnett**
    c. **Darrell Waltrip**
    d. **Dale Earnhardt**

303. In 1949, who won the first NASCAR premier series championship as crew chief?

    a. **Raymond Parks**
    b. **Red Vogt**
    c. **Smokey Yunick**
    d. **Bud Moore**

304. Which NASCAR premier series driver won the first series race ever held at Phoenix International Raceway?

    a. **Bill Elliott**
    b. **Davey Allison**
    c. **Alan Kulwicki**
    d. **Ricky Rudd**

305. Which car manufacturer has the most NASCAR premier series wins at Texas Motor Speedway since 1997?

    a. **Chevrolet**
    b. **Dodge**
    c. **Ford**
    d. **Toyota**

306. As of the beginning of the 2012 season, which driver has the most career NASCAR premier series victories at Darlington Raceway?

    a. **Bobby Allison**
    b. **Dale Eanrhardt**
    c. **Jeff Gordon**
    d. **David Pearson**

307. Who was the oldest driver to compete full-time in one of the top-3 NASCAR series in 2011?

    a. **Mark Martin**
    b. **Bobby Labonte**
    c. **Bill Elliott**
    d. **Morgan Shepherd**

308. Who was scheduled to try qualifying the No. 50 Walmart Chevrolet in a one-race sponsorship deal for the July 2012 Daytona race in the NASCAR Sprint Cup Series?

    a. **Jeff Gordon**
    b. **Bill Elliott**
    c. **Jimmie Johnson**
    d. **Tony Stewart**

309. At which track did David Stremme make his NASCAR premier series debut in 2005?

    a. **Chicagoland Speedway**
    b. **Sonoma**
    c. **Las Vegas Motor Speedway**
    d. **Michigan International Speedway**

310. As of the end of the 2011 NASCAR Camping World Truck Series season, which driver has won the most championships in the series?

    a. **Mike Skinner**
    b. **Jack Sprague**
    c. **Ron Hornaday Jr.**
    d. **Todd Bodine**

311. From which college did Ryan Newman graduate?

    a. **Purdue University**
    b. **Notre Dame**
    c. **Clemson University**
    d. **Indiana University**

312. Which NASCAR driver is a former member of the Georgetown University Hoyas basketball team?

    a. **Martin Truex Jr.**
    b. **Elliott Sadler**
    c. **Brendan Gaughan**
    d. **Cole Whitt**

313. Which NASCAR Nationwide Series driver played for the Waterloo Black Hawks?

    a. **Ricky Stenhouse Jr.**
    b. **Michael Annett**
    c. **Justin Allgaier**
    d. **Reed Sorenson**

314. Who was the youngest driver to claim the NASCAR premier series championship?

    a. **Bill Rexford**
    b. **Tim Flock**
    c. **Richard Petty**
    d. **Dale Earnhardt**

315. Which past NASCAR premier series champion was said to be able to see the air move over his car?

    a. **Junior Johnson**
    b. **Glen Wood**
    c. **Bill Elliott**
    d. **Dale Earnhardt**

316. As of the beginning of the 2012 season, which NASCAR premier series driver holds the record for the fastest average speed of 151.952 mph during the 600-mile race at Charlotte Motor Speedway?

    a. Jimmie Johnson
    b. Jeff Gordon
    c. Bobby Labonte
    d. Casey Mears

317. As of the end of the 2011 season, which driver holds the record for the most poles in a single season with 20?

    a. Bobby Isaac
    b. Ned Jarrett
    c. Richard Petty
    d. Tim Richmond

318. Which NASCAR premier series driver has the most victories from pole position?

    a. David Pearson
    b. Cale Yarborough
    c. Richard Petty
    d. Darrell Waltrip

319. Which NASCAR premier series driver has the most victories on superspeedways two miles or longer?

    a. **Jeff Gordon**
    b. **David Pearson**
    c. **Richard Petty**
    d. **Bobby Allison**

320. Which NASCAR premier series driver has the most victories on short tracks?

    a. **Kyle Busch**
    b. **Jeff Gordon**
    c. **Richard Petty**
    d. **David Pearson**

321. Which company sponsored Dale Jarrett when he won his first race in the NASCAR premier series?

    a. **UPS**
    b. **Hardee's**
    c. **Interstate Batteries**
    d. **Citgo**

322. Who owned the No. 40 Chevrolet that Bobby Allison raced in for the four races he competed in during the 1961 NASCAR premier series season?

    a. **Bobby Allison**
    b. **Ralph Stark**
    c. **Ed Grady**
    d. **Smokey Yunick**

323. When Carl Edwards won his first race in the NASCAR premier series, which company was sponsoring his Ford?

    a. **Office Depot**
    b. **Stonebridge Life Insurance**
    c. **Scotts**
    d. **Dish Network**

324. Which driver won the most races during the 1950 NASCAR premier series season?

    a. **Curtis Turner**
    b. **Dick Linder**
    c. **Fonty Flock**
    d. **Harold Kite**

325. As of the beginning of the 2012 season, the greatest margin of victory at Texas Motor Speedway in a NASCAR Sprint Cup Series race came on November 8, 2009, when Kurt Busch led which driver to the finish line by more than 25 seconds?

    a. **Denny Hamlin**
    b. **Carl Edwards**
    c. **Tony Stewart**
    d. **Jeff Gordon**

326. Who won the inaugural NASCAR Sprint Cup Series event at Kentucky Speedway on July 9, 2011?

    a. **Brad Keselowski**
    b. **Kurt Busch**
    c. **Kevin Harvick**
    d. **Kyle Busch**

327. Who was the first driver to give Roger Penske and Penske Racing its first win in the NASCAR premier series?

    a. **Dave Marcis**
    b. **Rusty Wallace**
    c. **Mark Donohue**
    d. **Bobby Allison**

328. Which NASCAR Sprint Cup Series regular teamed up with Oswaldo Negri, John Pew and Justin Wilson to win the 2012 Rolex 24 At Daytona?

    a. **Dale Earnhardt Jr.**
    b. **Robby Gordon**
    c. **AJ Allmendinger**
    d. **Juan Pablo Montoya**

329. Who won the Rookie of the Year in the NASCAR Camping World Truck Series in 1998 and then the Rookie of the Year in the NASCAR Nationwide Series in 2001?

    a. **Travis Kvapil**
    b. **Todd Bodine**
    c. **Greg Biffle**
    d. **Carl Edwards**

330. At which track did Dave Blaney earn his first pole in the NASCAR premier series?

    a. **Daytona International Speedway**
    b. **Rockingham Speedway**
    c. **Las Vegas Motor Speedway**
    d. **New Hampshire Motor Speedway**

331. Which short track in Ohio did a current NASCAR Sprint Cup Series driver buy in 2002?

a. Sharon Speedway
b. Kil-Kare Speedway
c. Limaland Motorsports Park
d. Columbus Motor Speedway

332. In 2007, Clint Bowyer won his first NASCAR Sprint Cup Series event at which track?

a. Sonoma
b. New Hampshire Motor Speedway
c. Dover International Speedway
d. Darlington Raceway

333. Which company sponsored the Richard Childress–owned Chevrolet Clint Bowyer drove to his first victory in the NASCAR Sprint Cup Series?

a. DIRECTV
b. Camping World
c. Jack Daniel's
d. BB&T

334. Which driver's pit crew won the 2011 NASCAR Sprint Pit Crew Challenge?

    a. Jeff Burton
    b. Jeff Gordon
    c. Denny Hamlin
    d. Jimmie Johnson

335. Which NASCAR Sprint Cup Series driver earned the first perfect Driver Rating (150.0) for a race?

    a. Jimmie Johnson
    b. Kyle Busch
    c. Kurt Busch
    d. Jeff Gordon

336. At which track did Kurt Busch earn his first victory in the NASCAR premier series?

    a. Bristol Motor Speedway
    b. Martinsville Speedway
    c. Atlanta Motor Speedway
    d. Homestead-Miami Speedway

337. Which track hosted the last NASCAR national touring series race to be run in the rain?

    a. **Watkins Glen International**
    b. **Richmond International Raceway**
    c. **Memphis Motorsport Park**
    d. **Circuit Gilles Villeneuve**

338. Which track, opened in 1990, was the first superspeedway built in the United States since 1969?

    a. **Las Vegas Motor Speedway**
    b. **Homestead-Miami Speedway**
    c. **New Hampshire Motor Speedway**
    d. **Kansas Speedway**

339. Which was the first track in NASCAR to use concrete?

    a. **Dover International Speedway**
    b. **Martinsville Speedway**
    c. **Bristol Motor Speedway**
    d. **Nashville Superspeedway**

340. Which past NASCAR premier series champion helped design Iowa Speedway in Newton?

    a. **Richard Petty**
    b. **Darrell Waltrip**
    c. **Rusty Wallace**
    d. **Bobby Allison**

341. Which current NASCAR Sprint Cup Series owner helped build Auto Club Speedway in Fontana, California?

    a. **Rick Hendrick**
    b. **Roger Penske**
    c. **Joe Gibbs**
    d. **Jack Roush**

342. Which track was the first west of the Mississippi River to host a NASCAR Nationwide Series race?

    a. **Las Vegas Motor Speedway**
    b. **Texas Motor Speedway**
    c. **Pikes Peak International Raceway**
    d. **Auto Club Speedway**

343. At which track did Dale Earnhardt Jr. earn his first victory in the NASCAR Nationwide Series?

    a. **Richmond International Raceway**
    b. **Daytona International Speedway**
    c. **Talladega Superspeedway**
    d. **Texas Motor Speedway**

344. Which track hosted the first race in the Chase for the NASCAR Sprint Cup in 2011?

    a. **New Hampshire Motor Speedway**
    b. **Chicagoland Speedway**
    c. **Richmond International Raceway**
    d. **Dover International Speedway**

345. In which race did Joe Gibbs earn his first victory as an owner in the NASCAR premier series?

    a. **2000 Allstate 400 at the Brickyard**
    b. **1995 Coca-Cola 600**
    c. **1996 NAPA 500**
    d. **1993 Daytona 500**

346. How many drivers does NASCAR guarantee a spot on a NASCAR Sprint Cup Series race's starting grid?

    a. 10
    b. 12
    c. 35
    d. 43

347. Which driver posted the largest margin of victory in the NASCAR premier series history?

    a. **Ned Jarrett**
    b. **Richard Petty**
    c. **Buck Baker**
    d. **Bill Elliott**

348. In which year were in-car cameras first used to get a driver's view of the track during a race?

    a. 1979
    b. 1983
    c. 1988
    d. 1992

349. Which current NASCAR Sprint Cup Series driver performs a celebratory back flip from the edge of his race car's window after a victory?

    a. Kyle Busch
    b. Carl Edwards
    c. Brad Keselowski
    d. Juan Pablo Montoya

350. Which driver won the NASCAR Modified Tour championship in its second year?

    a. Jerry Cook
    b. Richie Evans
    c. Fonty Flock
    d. Lee Petty

351. Which of the following NASCAR premier series champions did not win the NASCAR Modified Tour championship?

    a. Joe Weatherly
    b. Bobby Allison
    c. Red Byron
    d. Bill Rexford

352. As of the end of the 2011 season, who had won a record three NASCAR Toyota Series championships, which is held in Mexico?

    a. **German Quiroga**
    b. **Antonio Perez**
    c. **Jorge Goeters**
    d. **Cesar Tiberio**

353. Which driver won the championship in the inaugural season of the NASCAR Canadian Tire Series?

    a. **Scott Steckly**
    b. **Patrick Carpentier**
    c. **Andrew Ranger**
    d. **DJ Kennington**

354. Which current NASCAR Sprint Cup Series regular won the NASCAR K&N Pro Series West championship in 1998?

    a. **Kurt Busch**
    b. **Jimmie Johnson**
    c. **Kevin Harvick**
    d. **Kasey Kahne**

355. Which did Kyle Busch learn to do during the 2006–07 off-season?

    a. **Make Sushi**
    b. **Massage**
    c. **Surf**
    d. **Play Guitar**

356. Who did Danica Patrick drive for part-time in the NASCAR Nationwide Series in 2010 and 2011?

    a. **Tony Stewart**
    b. **Dale Earnhardt Jr.**
    c. **Rick Hendrick**
    d. **Roger Penske**

357. At which track did Dale Earnhardt Jr. win his first pole in the NASCAR premier series?

    a. **Charlotte Motor Speedway**
    b. **Michigan International Speedway**
    c. **Texas Motor Speedway**
    d. **Kansas Speedway**

358. Who won the Rookie of the Year in the NASCAR Camping World Truck Series in 2003 and then went on to win the same award in the NASCAR Nationwide Series two years later?

    a. **Carl Edwards**
    b. **Kasey Kahne**
    c. **Greg Biffle**
    d. **Kyle Busch**

359. Which job did Carl Edwards have before signing with Roush Fenway Racing?

    a. **Janitor**
    b. **Substitute Teacher**
    c. **Fitness Instructor**
    d. **Store Manager**

360. Who won the pole for the 2007 Daytona 500?

    a. **Ryan Newman**
    b. **Jimmie Johnson**
    c. **Matt Kenseth**
    d. **David Gilliland**

361. In 1994, who won his first NASCAR premier series race at Charlotte Motor Speedway after starting from the pole?

    a. **Bobby Labonte**
    b. **Jeff Green**
    c. **Jeff Gordon**
    d. **Sterling Marlin**

362. Which NASCAR Sprint Cup Series driver has qualified for every Chase for the NASCAR Sprint Cup since the new format was implemented before the 2004 season?

    a. **Tony Stewart**
    b. **Jimmie Johnson**
    c. **Jeff Gordon**
    d. **Denny Hamlin**

363. Which driver scored Kevin Harvick Inc.'s first win in the NASCAR Camping World Truck Series?

    a. **Ron Hornaday Jr.**
    b. **Nelson Piquet Jr.**
    c. **Kevin Harvick**
    d. **Elliott Sadler**

364. At which track did Kevin Harvick win his first pole in the NASCAR premier series?

    a. **Daytona International Speedway**
    b. **New Hampshire Motor Speedway**
    c. **Richmond International Raceway**
    d. **Talladega Superspeedway**

365. Who was the last driver-owner to take his race car to Victory Lane before Tony Stewart won in 2009, driving for Stewart-Haas Racing?

    a. **Alan Kulwicki**
    b. **Ricky Rudd**
    c. **Michael Waltrip**
    d. **Robby Gordon**

366. Which NASCAR premier series driver won twice at Dover International Speedway during his rookie campaign?

    a. **Bobby Allison**
    b. **Ryan Newman**
    c. **Tony Stewart**
    d. **Jimmie Johnson**

367. At which track did Jimmie Johnson capture his first victory in the NASCAR premier series?

    a. **Dover International Speedway**
    b. **New Hampshire Motor Speedway**
    c. **Auto Club Speedway**
    d. **Pocono Raceway**

368. For which team did Kasey Kahne drive full-time during the 2011 NASCAR Sprint Cup Series season?

    a. **Hendrick Motorsports**
    b. **Richard Petty Motorsports**
    c. **Red Bull Racing**
    d. **Stewart-Haas Racing**

369. Who designed the 2007 NASCAR Day lapel pin that fans could purchase from The NASCAR Foundation?

    a. **Betty Jane France**
    b. **Sam Bass**
    c. **Mike Helton**
    d. **Kyle Petty**

370. Which of the following celebrities has not been a NASCAR Day spokesperson?

    a. Keith Urban
    b. Will Ferrell
    c. Kelly Clarkson
    d. Garth Brooks

371. At which track did Kasey Kahne win his first race in the NASCAR premier series?

    a. Atlanta Motor Speedway
    b. Texas Motor Speedway
    c. Charlotte Motor Speedway
    d. Richmond International Raceway

372. At which track did Matt Kenseth win his first race in the NASCAR premier series?

    a. Auto Club Speedway
    b. Charlotte Motor Speedway
    c. Texas Motor Speedway
    d. Rockingham Speedway

373. How many starts in the NASCAR Sprint Cup Series did it take before Brad Keselowski won a race?

    a. **One**
    b. **Three**
    c. **Five**
    d. **Seven**

374. Through the 2011 season, which driver has the most wins in the Chase for the NASCAR Sprint Cup with 20 trips to Victory Lane during NASCAR's playoffs?

    a. **Jimmie Johnson**
    b. **Tony Stewart**
    c. **Carl Edwards**
    d. **Greg Biffle**

375. Who won the first ever race in the Chase for the NASCAR Sprint Cup?

    a. **Dale Earnhardt Jr.**
    b. **Kurt Busch**
    c. **Tony Stewart**
    d. **Ryan Newman**

376. Which driver broke the track qualifying record at New Hampshire Motor Speedway to win his first career pole?

    a. Brian Vickers
    b. Ernie Irvan
    c. Brad Keselowski
    d. Ryan Newman

377. Which NASCAR driver appeared on an episode of *The Guiding Light*?

    a. Tim Richmond
    b. David Ragan
    c. Travis Kvapil
    d. Jeff Gordon

378. As of the beginning of the 2012 season, at which track did Bobby Labonte earn his last trip to Victory Lane in the NASCAR premier series?

    a. Michigan International Speedway
    b. Homestead-Miami Speedway
    c. Atlanta Motor Speedway
    d. Talladega Superspeedway

379. Which NASCAR Sprint Cup Series driver holds the record for being the youngest pole winner in the series at 19 years, 9 months and 25 days?

    a. Kyle Busch
    b. Brad Keselowski
    c. Joey Logano
    d. David Ragan

380. Which NASCAR driver is the oldest pole winner in the NASCAR premier series at 54 years, 7 months and 17 days?

    a. Harry Gant
    b. Mark Martin
    c. Dick Trickle
    d. Richard Petty

381. In 1981, Mark Martin earned his first pole in the NASCAR premier series. At which track did he claim his first pole?

    a. Richmond International Raceway
    b. Rockingham Speedway
    c. Nashville Speedway
    d. Michigan International Speedway

382. Who holds the distinction of being the 100th individual driver to win in the NASCAR Nationwide Series?

    a. **Jamie McMurray**
    b. **Jason Keller**
    c. **Jack Sprague**
    d. **Johnny Sauter**

383. In 2002, at which track did Jamie McMurray secure his first NASCAR premier series victory?

    a. **Talladega Superspeedway**
    b. **Charlotte Motor Speedway**
    c. **Atlanta Motor Speedway**
    d. **Phoenix International Raceway**

384. Which driver won the 100th NASCAR Camping World Truck Series event?

    a. **Mike Wallace**
    b. **Greg Biffle**
    c. **Ron Hornaday Jr.**
    d. **Jack Sprague**

385. Who was the first full-time NASCAR Sprint Cup Series driver to score the overall win in the Rolex 24 At Daytona?

    a. AJ Allmendinger
    b. Jimmie Johnson
    c. Juan Pablo Montoya
    d. Casey Mears

386. At which track did Paul Menard earn his only pole in the NASCAR Sprint Cup Series (as of the start of the 2012 season)?

    a. Kansas Speedway
    b. Talladega Superspeedway
    c. Daytona International Speedway
    d. Phoenix International Raceway

387. Which Florida college did Joe Nemechek attend?

    a. Florida Institute of Technology
    b. Stetson University
    c. Florida Atlantic University
    d. Florida Agricultural and Mechanical University

388. At which track did Joe Nemechek earn his first NASCAR premier series victory?

    a. **Rockingham Speedway**
    b. **Richmond International Raceway**
    c. **Kansas Speedway**
    d. **New Hampshire Motor Speedway**

389. Which of the following NASCAR drivers appeared in a music video for the rock band 3 Doors Down?

    a. **Tony Stewart**
    b. **Scott Speed**
    c. **Kyle Busch**
    d. **Carl Edwards**

390. Which of the following drivers was named one of *USA Weekend Magazine*'s 2004 Most Caring Athletes?

    a. **Jeff Gordon**
    b. **Tony Stewart**
    c. **Dale Earnhardt Jr.**
    d. **Mark Martin**

391. At which track did Tony Stewart win his first race in the NASCAR premier series?

    a. **Homestead-Miami Speedway**
    b. **Richmond International Raceway**
    c. **Martinsville Speedway**
    d. **New Hampshire Motor Speedway**

392. Who is the youngest driver to win a championship in one of NASCAR's national touring series?

    a. **Kyle Busch**
    b. **Austin Dillon**
    c. **Brian Vickers**
    d. **Ricky Stenhouse Jr.**

393. At which track did Brian Vickers win his first NASCAR premier series race?

    a. **Talladega Superspeedway**
    b. **Michigan International Speedway**
    c. **Richmond International Raceway**
    d. **Chicagoland Speedway**

394. At which track did J.J. Yeley earn his first pole in the NASCAR Sprint Cup Series?

    a. **Phoenix International Raceway**
    b. **Charlotte Motor Speedway**
    c. **Kansas Speedway**
    d. **Michigan International Speedway**

395. At which track did Robby Gordon win his first race in the NASCAR premier series?

    a. **Auto Club Speedway**
    b. **Watkins Glen International**
    c. **Sonoma**
    d. **New Hampshire Motor Speedway**

396. Which former NASCAR driver was offered a full university golf scholarship?

    a. **Dale Jarrett**
    b. **Cale Yarborough**
    c. **Darrell Waltrip**
    d. **Ernie Irvan**

397. In 2011, which crew chief was named the DIRECTV Crew Chief of the Year?

    a. **Chad Knaus**
    b. **Bob Osborne**
    c. **Gil Martin**
    d. **Steve Addington**

398. In 2011, which pit crew won the Mechanix Wear Most Valuable Pit Crew Award?

    a. **No. 99 Roush Fenway Racing Team**
    b. **No. 11 Joe Gibbs Racing Team**
    c. **No. 48 Hendrick Motorsports Team**
    d. **No. 2 Penske Racing Team**

399. In 2011, which NASCAR Sprint Cup Series driver won the season-ending Mobil 1 Driver of the Race Award?

    a. **Kevin Harvick**
    b. **Kyle Busch**
    c. **Carl Edwards**
    d. **Tony Stewart**

400. In 1938, Bill France Sr. promoted his first race with the help of friend and nightclub owner Charlie Reese, who provided the financial resources. How much profit did France and Reese make from their first attempt at promoting a stock car race?

    a. $0
    b. $100
    c. $200
    d. $700

401. At which track did Janet Guthrie lead a lap in a NASCAR premier series race, making her the only female driver to lead a race in the series as of the beginning of the 2012 season?

    a. **Ontario Motor Speedway**
    b. **Daytona International Speedway**
    c. **Richmond International Raceway**
    d. **Nashville Speedway**

402. Which driver founded Charlotte Motor Speedway with Bruton Smith?

    a. **Lee Petty**
    b. **Junior Johnson**
    c. **Ned Jarrett**
    d. **Curtis Turner**

403. As of the beginning of the 2012 season, which driver has the most career wins in the NASCAR premier series at Atlanta Motor Speedway?

   a. **Cale Yarborough**
   b. **Dale Earnhardt**
   c. **Bobby Labonte**
   d. **Richard Petty**

404. As of the beginning of the 2012 season, which current driver is tied with Buddy Baker for the most career poles in the NASCAR premier series at Atlanta Motor Speedway?

   a. **Jeff Gordon**
   b. **Dale Earnhardt Jr.**
   c. **Bill Elliott**
   d. **Ryan Newman**

405. As of the beginning of the 2012 season, which driver holds the NASCAR premier series qualifying record at Atlanta Motor Speedway with a speed of 197.478 mph?

   a. **Geoff Bodine**
   b. **Ryan Newman**
   c. **Alan Kulwicki**
   d. **David Pearson**

406. As of the beginning of the 2012 season, which driver holds the NASCAR premier series race record at Atlanta Motor Speedway with a speed of 159.904 mph?

    a. **Bobby Labonte**
    b. **Jeff Gordon**
    c. **Richard Petty**
    d. **Harry Gant**

407. As of the beginning of the 2012 season, which team has the most NASCAR premier series victories at Atlanta Motor Speedway?

    a. **Hendrick Motorsports**
    b. **Richard Childress Racing**
    c. **Wood Brothers**
    d. **Petty Enterprises**

408. As of the beginning of the 2012 season, which driver has the most career wins in the NASCAR premier series at Auto Club Speedway?

    a. **Jimmie Johnson**
    b. **Jeff Gordon**
    c. **Kevin Harvick**
    d. **Matt Kenseth**

409. As of the beginning of the 2012 season, which driver has the most career poles in the NASCAR premier series at Auto Club Speedway?

a. Brian Vickers
b. Juan Pablo Montoya
c. Jamie McMurray
d. Kurt Busch

410. As of the beginning of the 2012 season, which driver holds the NASCAR premier series qualifying record at Auto Club Speedway with a speed of 188.245 mph?

a. Kyle Busch
b. Denny Hamlin
c. Ryan Newman
d. Carl Edwards

411. As of the beginning of the 2012 season, which driver holds the NASCAR premier series race record at Auto Club Speedway with a speed of 155.012 mph?

a. Matt Kenseth
b. Jimmie Johnson
c. Jeff Gordon
d. Kevin Harvick

412. As of the beginning of the 2012 season, which driver has the most career wins in the NASCAR premier series at Bristol Motor Speedway?

    a. **Darrell Waltrip**
    b. **Kyle Busch**
    c. **Rusty Wallace**
    d. **Cale Yarborough**

413. As of the beginning of the 2012 season, which team has the most NASCAR premier series victories at Bristol Motor Speedway?

    a. **Penske Racing**
    b. **Petty Motorsports**
    c. **Roush Fenway Racing**
    d. **Junior Johnson Racing**

414. As of the beginning of the 2012 season, which current driver is tied with Cale Yarborough for the most career poles in the NASCAR premier series at Bristol Motor Speedway?

    a. **Ryan Newman**
    b. **Kurt Busch**
    c. **Mark Martin**
    d. **Jeff Gordon**

415. As of the beginning of 2012 season, which driver holds the NASCAR premier series qualifying record at Bristol Motor Speedway with a speed of 128.709 mph?

    a. **David Pearson**
    b. **Ryan Newman**
    c. **Dale Earnhardt**
    d. **Ernie Irvan**

416. As of the beginning of the 2012 season, which driver holds the NASCAR premier series race record at Bristol Motor Speedway with a speed of 101.074 mph?

    a. **Carl Edwards**
    b. **Cale Yarborough**
    c. **Charlie Glotzbach**
    d. **Terry Labonte**

417. As of the beginning of the 2012 season, which current driver is tied with Bobby Allison and Darrell Waltrip for the most career points wins in the NASCAR premier series at Charlotte Motor Speedway?

    a. **Jimmie Johnson**
    b. **Jeff Gordon**
    c. **Jeff Burton**
    d. **Mark Martin**

418. As of the beginning of the 2012 season, which team has the most NASCAR premier series points-earning victories at Charlotte Motor Speedway?

    a. **Holman Moody**
    b. **Petty Enterprises**
    c. **Hendrick Motorsports**
    d. **Junior Johnson Racing**

419. As of the beginning of the 2012 season, which driver has the most career poles in the NASCAR premier series at Charlotte Motor Speedway?

    a. **Bill Elliott**
    b. **David Pearson**
    c. **Ryan Newman**
    d. **Jeff Gordon**

420. As of the beginning of the 2012 season, which driver holds the NASCAR premier series qualifying record at Charlotte Motor Speedway with a speed of 193.216 mph?

    a. **Fred Lorenzen**
    b. **Elliott Sadler**
    c. **Neil Bonnett**
    d. **Ken Schrader**

421. As of the beginning of the 2012 season, which driver holds the NASCAR premier series race record for a 500-mile event at Charlotte Motor Speedway with a speed of 160.306 mph?

    a. **Jeff Gordon**
    b. **Matt Kenseth**
    c. **Tony Stewart**
    d. **Donnie Allison**

422. As of the beginning of the 2012 season, which driver has the most career wins in the NASCAR premier series at Chicagoland Speedway?

    a. **Tony Stewart**
    b. **Kevin Harvick**
    c. **Dale Earnhardt Jr.**
    d. **David Reutimann**

423. As of the beginning of the 2012 season, which team has the most NASCAR premier series victories at Chicagoland Speedway?

    a. **Joe Gibbs Racing**
    b. **Stewart-Haas Racing**
    c. **Richard Childress Racing**
    d. **Hendrick Motorsports**

424. As of the beginning of the 2012 season, which driver holds the NASCAR premier series qualifying record at Chicagoland Speedway with a speed of 188.147 mph?

    a. **Casey Mears**
    b. **Todd Bodine**
    c. **Jeff Gordon**
    d. **Jimmie Johnson**

425. As of the beginning of the 2012 season, which driver holds the NASCAR premier series race record at Chicagoland Speedway with a speed of 145.138 mph?

    a. **Ryan Newman**
    b. **David Reutimann**
    c. **Tony Stewart**
    d. **Kevin Harvick**

426. As of the beginning of the 2012 season, which driver has the most career poles in the NASCAR premier series at Darlington Raceway?

    a. **Bill Elliott**
    b. **Glenn "Fireball" Roberts**
    c. **Fred Lorenzen**
    d. **David Pearson**

427. As of the beginning of 2012 season, which team has the most NASCAR premier series victories at Darlington Raceway?

    a. **Hendrick Motorsports**
    b. **Junior Johnson Racing**
    c. **Holman Moody**
    d. **Richard Childress Racing**

428. As of the beginning of the 2012 season, which driver holds the NASCAR premier series qualifying record at Darlington Raceway with a speed of 181.254 mph?

    a. **Greg Biffle**
    b. **Kasey Kahne**
    c. **Ricky Rudd**
    d. **Mark Martin**

429. As of the beginning of the 2012 season, which driver holds the NASCAR premier series race record at Darlington Raceway with a speed of 140.350 mph?

    a. **Dale Earnhardt**
    b. **Jeff Gordon**
    c. **Kyle Busch**
    d. **Harry Gant**

430. As of the beginning of the 2012 season, which driver has the most career poles in the NASCAR premier series at Daytona International Speedway?

    a. **Mark Martin**
    b. **Cale Yarborough**
    c. **Sterling Marlin**
    d. **Glenn "Fireball" Roberts**

431. As of the beginning of the 2012 season, which driver has the most career points wins in the NASCAR premier series at Daytona International Speedway?

    a. **Richard Petty**
    b. **Jeff Gordon**
    c. **David Pearson**
    d. **Dale Jarrett**

432. As of the beginning of the 2012 season, which team has the most NASCAR premier series points-earning wins at Daytona International Speedway?

    a. **Hendrick Motorsports**
    b. **Petty Enterprises**
    c. **Wood Brothers**
    d. **DEI**

433. As of the beginning of the 2012 season, which driver holds the NASCAR premier series race record for a 400-mile event at Daytona International Speedway with a speed of 173.473 mph?

    a. **Bobby Allison**
    b. **Richard Petty**
    c. **Junior Johnson**
    d. **Bobby Isaac**

434. As of the beginning of the 2012 season, which driver holds the NASCAR premier series race record for a 500-mile event at Daytona International Speedway with a speed of 177.602 mph?

    a. **Cale Yarborough**
    b. **Dale Earnhardt**
    c. **Bill Elliott**
    d. **Buddy Baker**

435. As of the beginning of the 2012 season, which driver has the most career poles in the NASCAR premier series at Dover International Speedway?

    a. **Rusty Wallace**
    b. **David Pearson**
    c. **Jimmie Johsnon**
    d. **Jeff Gordon**

436. As of the beginning of the 2012 season, which two drivers have the most career wins in the NASCAR premier series at Dover International Speedway?

    a. **Jimmie Johnson and Richard Petty**
    b. **Bobby Allison and Richard Petty**
    c. **Bobby Allison and David Pearson**
    d. **Jimmie Johnson and David Pearson**

437. As of the beginning of the 2012 season, which team has the most NASCAR premier series wins at Dover International Speedway?

    a. **Penske Racing**
    b. **Wood Brothers**
    c. **Roush Fenway Racing**
    d. **Hendrick Motorsports**

438. As of the beginning of the 2012 season, which driver holds the NASCAR premier series qualifying record at Dover International Speedway with a speed of 161.522 mph?

    a. **Mark Martin**
    b. **David Pearson**
    c. **Jeremy Mayfield**
    d. **Rick Mast**

439. As of the beginning of the 2012 season, which driver holds the NASCAR premier series race record at Dover International Speedway with a speed of 132.719 mph?

    a. **Derrike Cope**
    b. **Mark Martin**
    c. **Jimmie Johnson**
    d. **Bill Elliott**

440. As of the beginning of the 2012 season, which of the following drivers has only one NASCAR premier series pole at Homestead-Miami Speedway?

    a. **Carl Edwards**
    b. **Kurt Busch**
    c. **Jamie McMurray**
    d. **Kasey Kahne**

441. As of the beginning of the 2012 season, which driver is tied with Tony Stewart for the most career wins in the NASCAR premier series at Homestead-Miami Speedway?

    a. **Greg Biffle**
    b. **Jimmie Johnson**
    c. **Carl Edwards**
    d. **Denny Hamlin**

442. As of the beginning of the 2012 season, which driver holds the NASCAR premier series qualifying record at Homestead-Miami Speedway with a speed of 181.111 mph?

    a. **David Reutimann**
    b. **Jamie McMurray**
    c. **Steve Park**
    d. **Carl Edwards**

443. As of the beginning of the 2012 season, which driver holds the NASCAR premier series race record at Homestead-Miami Speedway with a speed of 140.335 mph?

    a. **Greg Biffle**
    b. **Matt Kenseth**
    c. **Carl Edwards**
    d. **Tony Stewart**

444. As of the beginning of the 2012 season, which driver has the most career poles in the NASCAR premier series at Indianapolis Motor Speedway?

    a. **Jeff Gordon**
    b. **Ernie Irvan**
    c. **David Ragan**
    d. **Reed Sorenson**

445. As of the beginning of the 2012 season, which driver has the most career wins in the NASCAR premier series at Indianapolis Motor Speedway?

    a. Jimmie Johnson
    b. Jeff Gordon
    c. Tony Stewart
    d. Dale Jarrett

446. As of the beginning of the 2012 season, which driver holds the NASCAR premier series qualifying record at Indianapolis Motor Speedway with a speed of 186.293 mph?

    a. Kevin Harvick
    b. Juan Pablo Montoya
    c. Tony Stewart
    d. Casey Mears

447. As of the beginning of the 2012 season, which driver holds the NASCAR premier series race record at Indianapolis Motor Speedway with a speed of 155.912 mph?

    a. Dale Earnhardt
    b. Dale Jarrett
    c. Jimmie Johnson
    d. Bobby Labonte

448. As of the beginning of the 2012 season, which driver has the most career poles in the NASCAR premier series at Sonoma?

    a. Jeff Gordon
    b. Kasey Kahne
    c. Kurt Busch
    d. Ricky Rudd

449. As of the beginning of the 2012 season, which driver has the most career wins in the NASCAR premier series at Sonoma?

    a. Ernie Irvan
    b. Rusty Wallace
    c. Tony Stewart
    d. Jeff Gordon

450. As of the beginning of the 2012 season, which driver holds the NASCAR premier series qualifying record at Sonoma with a speed of 94.325 mph?

    a. Ricky Rudd
    b. Terry Labonte
    c. Rusty Wallace
    d. Jeff Gordon

451. As of the beginning of the 2012 season, which driver holds the NASCAR premier series race record on Sonoma's current track configuration with a speed of 81.007 mph?

    a. Jeff Gordon
    b. Ricky Rudd
    c. Ernie Irvan
    d. Rusty Wallace

452. As of the beginning of the 2012 season, which driver has the most career poles in the NASCAR premier series at Kansas Speedway?

    a. Kasey Kahne
    b. Jimmie Johnson
    c. Dale Earnhardt Jr.
    d. Kurt Busch

453. As of the beginning of the 2012 season, which of the following drivers has one win in the NASCAR premier series at Kansas Speedway versus the two wins the other three have at the track?

    a. Ryan Newman
    b. Jimmie Johnson
    c. Greg Biffle
    d. Tony Stewart

454. As of the beginning of the 2012 season, which driver holds the NASCAR premier series qualifying record at Kansas Speedway with a speed of 180.856 mph?

    a. Joe Nemechek
    b. Jimmie Johnson
    c. Jason Leffler
    d. Matt Kenseth

455. As of the beginning of the 2012 season, which driver holds the NASCAR premier series race record at Kansas Speedway with a speed of 138.077 mph?

    a. Mark Martin
    b. Tony Stewart
    c. Greg Biffle
    d. Brad Keselowski

456. Which driver posted the fastest qualifying speed to win the pole for the inaugural NASCAR Sprint Cup Series race at Kentucky Speedway in 2011?

    a. Kyle Busch
    b. Kurt Busch
    c. Juan Pablo Montoya
    d. Qualifying was cancelled

457. As of the beginning of the 2012 season, which team has the most NASCAR premier series victories at Las Vegas Motor Speedway?

    a. **Hendrick Motorsports**
    b. **Roush Fenway Racing**
    c. **Joe Gibbs Racing**
    d. **DEI**

458. As of the beginning of the 2012 season, which driver has the most career wins in the NASCAR premier series at Las Vegas Motor Speedway?

    a. **Carl Edwards**
    b. **Matt Kenseth**
    c. **Jimmie Johnson**
    d. **Jeff Burton**

459. As of the end of the 2012 season, which driver holds the NASCAR premier series qualifying record at Las Vegas Motor Speedway with a speed of 190.456?

    a. **Kasey Kahne**
    b. **Matt Kenseth**
    c. **Bobby Labonte**
    d. **Ryan Newman**

460. As of the beginning of the 2012 season, which driver holds the NASCAR premier series race record at Las Vegas Motor Speedway with a speed of 146.554 mph?

    a. Jimmie Johnson
    b. Sterling Marlin
    c. Jeff Burton
    d. Mark Martin

461. As of the beginning of the 2012 season, which driver has the most career wins in the NASCAR premier series at Martinsville Speedway?

    a. Darrell Waltrip
    b. Jeff Gordon
    c. Richard Petty
    d. Rusty Wallace

462. As of the beginning of the 2012 season, which driver has the most career poles in the NASCAR premier series at Martinsville Speedway?

    a. Buck Baker
    b. Darrell Waltrip
    c. Jeff Gordon
    d. Geoff Bodine

463. As of the beginning of the 2012 season, which team has the most NASCAR premier series victories at Martinsville Speedway?

    a. **Joe Gibbs Racing**
    b. **Petty Enterprises**
    c. **Hendrick Motorsports**
    d. **Junior Johnson Racing**

464. As of the beginning of the 2012 season, which driver holds the NASCAR premier series qualifying record at Martinsville Speedway with a speed of 98.083 mph?

    a. **Tony Stewart**
    b. **Cale Yarborough**
    c. **Dale Earnhardt**
    d. **Mark Martin**

465. As of the beginning of the 2012 season, which driver holds the NASCAR premier series race record at Martinsville Speedway with a speed of 82.223 mph?

    a. **Jeff Gordon**
    b. **Rusty Wallace**
    c. **Cale Yarborough**
    d. **Darrell Waltrip**

466. As of the beginning of the 2012 season, which driver has the most career poles in the NASCAR premier series at Michigan International Speedway?

    a. **Bobby Labonte**
    b. **Bill Elliott**
    c. **Jeff Gordon**
    d. **David Pearson**

467. As of the beginning of the 2012 season, which driver has the most career wins in the NASCAR premier series at Michigan International Speedway?

    a. **Mark Martin**
    b. **Cale Yarborough**
    c. **David Pearson**
    d. **Bill Elliott**

468. As of the beginning of the 2012 season, which driver holds the NASCAR premier series qualifying record at Michigan International Speedway with a speed of 194.232?

    a. **Ryan Newman**
    b. **Brian Vickers**
    c. **Kasey Kahne**
    d. **David Pearson**

469. As of the beginning of the 2012 season, which driver holds the NASCAR premier series race record at Michigan International Speedway with a speed of 173.997?

    a. **Dale Jarrett**
    b. **Davey Allison**
    c. **Rusty Wallace**
    d. **Denny Hamlin**

470. As of the beginning of the 2012 season, which driver has the most career wins in the NASCAR premier series at New Hampshire Motor Speedway?

    a. **Kurt Busch**
    b. **Ryan Newman**
    c. **Tony Stewart**
    d. **Jeff Burton**

471. As of the beginning of the 2012 season, which driver has the most career poles in the NASCAR premier series at New Hampshire Motor Speedway?

    a. **Jeff Gordon**
    b. **Ricky Craven**
    c. **Ryan Newman**
    d. **Juan Pablo Montoya**

472. As of the beginning of the 2012 season, which driver holds the NASCAR premier series race record at New Hampshire Motor Speedway with a speed of 117.134 mph?

    a. Jeff Burton
    b. Tony Stewart
    c. Jimmie Johnson
    d. Jeff Gordon

473. As of the beginning of the 2012 season, which driver holds the NASCAR premier series qualifying record at New Hampshire Motor Speedway with a speed of 135.232 mph?

    a. Juan Pablo Montoya
    b. Brad Keselowski
    c. Ryan Newman
    d. Kevin Harvick

474. As of the beginning of the 2012 season, which driver has the most career poles in the NASCAR premier series at Phoenix International Raceway?

    a. Carl Edwards
    b. Ryan Newman
    c. Jeff Gordon
    d. Rusty Wallace

475. As of the beginning of the 2012 season, which driver has the most career wins in the NASCAR premier series at Phoenix International Raceway?

    a. **Davey Allison**
    b. **Jimmie Johnson**
    c. **Kevin Harvick**
    d. **Dale Earnhardt Jr.**

476. As of the beginning of the 2012 season, which driver holds the NASCAR premier series qualifying record at Phoenix International Raceway with a speed of 137.279 mph?

    a. **Carl Edwards**
    b. **Jimmie Johnson**
    c. **Mark Martin**
    d. **Jeff Gordon**

477. As of the beginning of the 2012 season, which driver holds the NASCAR premier series race record at Phoenix International Raceway with a speed of 118.132 mph?

    a. **Matt Kenseth**
    b. **Kasey Kahne**
    c. **Dale Jarrett**
    d. **Tony Stewart**

478. As of the beginning of the 2012 season, which driver is tied with Bill Elliott for the most career poles in the NASCAR premier series at Pocono Raceway?

    a. **Darrell Waltrip**
    b. **Mark Martin**
    c. **Ken Schrader**
    d. **Cale Yarborough**

479. As of the beginning of the 2012 season, which driver is tied with Bill Elliott for the most career wins in the NASCAR premier series at Pocono Raceway?

    a. **Jeff Gordon**
    b. **Tim Richmond**
    c. **Denny Hamlin**
    d. **Rusty Wallace**

480. As of the beginning of the 2012 season, which driver holds the NASCAR premier series qualifying record at Pocono Raceway with a speed of 172.533 mph?

    a. **Tony Stewart**
    b. **Kasey Kahne**
    c. **Denny Hamlin**
    d. **Bill Elliott**

481. As of the beginning of the 2012 season, which driver holds the NASCAR premier series race record at Pocono Raceway with a speed of 145.384 mph?

    a. **Dale Jarrett**
    b. **Rusty Wallace**
    c. **Jeff Gordon**
    d. **Alan Kulwicki**

482. As of the beginning of the 2012 season, which driver has the most career wins in the NASCAR premier series at Richmond International Raceway?

    a. **Dale Earnhardt**
    b. **Richard Petty**
    c. **Darrell Waltrip**
    d. **David Pearson**

483. As of the beginning of the 2012 season, which driver is tied with Richard Petty for the most career poles in the NASCAR premier series at Richmond International Raceway?

    a. **Ned Jarrett**
    b. **Bobby Allison**
    c. **Jeff Gordon**
    d. **Darrell Waltrip**

484. As of the beginning of the 2012 season, which team has the most victories in the NASCAR premier series at Richmond International Raceway?

   a. **Hendrick Motorsports**
   b. **Junior Johnson Racing**
   c. **Richard Childress Racing**
   d. **Petty Enterprises**

485. As of the beginning of the 2012 season, which driver holds the NASCAR premier series qualifying record at Richmond International Raceway with a speed of 129.983 mph?

   a. **Brian Vickers**
   b. **Geoff Bodine**
   c. **Denny Hamlin**
   d. **Jeff Gordon**

486. As of the beginning of the 2012 season, which driver holds the NASCAR premier series race record at Richmond International Raceway with a speed of 109.047 mph?

   a. **Dale Jarrett**
   b. **Kasey Kahne**
   c. **Kevin Harvick**
   d. **Rusty Wallace**

487. As of the beginning of the 2012 season, which driver has the most career poles in the NASCAR premier series at Talladega Superspeedway?

    a. **Bobby Isaac**
    b. **Cale Yarborough**
    c. **Bill Elliott**
    d. **Ernie Irvan**

488. As of the beginning of the 2012 season, which driver has the most career wins in the NASCAR premier series at Talladega Superspeedway?

    a. **Buddy Baker**
    b. **Dale Earnhardt Jr.**
    c. **Jeff Gordon**
    d. **Dale Earnhardt**

489. As of the beginning of the 2012 season, which team has the most victories in the NASCAR premier series at Talladega Superspeedway?

    a. **Hendrick Motorsports**
    b. **Petty Enterprises**
    c. **DEI**
    d. **Richard Childress Racing**

490. As of the beginning of the 2012 season, which driver holds the NASCAR premier series race record at Talladega Superspeedway with a speed of 188.354 mph?

   a. **Bobby Hamilton**
   b. **Mark Martin**
   c. **Dale Earnhardt Jr.**
   d. **Bill Elliott**

491. As of the beginning of the 2012 season, which of the following drivers has only one pole in the NASCAR premier series at Texas Motor Speedway, rather than the two poles the other three drivers have at the track?

   a. **Ryan Newman**
   b. **Kenny Irwin Jr.**
   c. **Bobby Labonte**
   d. **Dale Earnhardt Jr.**

492. As of the beginning of the 2012 season, which team has the most victories in the NASCAR premier series at Texas Motor Speedway?

   a. **Roush Fenway Racing**
   b. **Penske Racing**
   c. **Hendrick Motorsports**
   d. **Joe Gibbs Racing**

493. As of the beginning of the 2012 season, which driver holds the NASCAR premier series qualifying record at Texas Motor Speedway with a speed of 196.235 mph?

    a. **Kasey Kahne**
    b. **Matt Kenseth**
    c. **Carl Edwards**
    d. **Brian Vickers**

494. As of the beginning of the 2012 season, which driver holds the NASCAR premier series race record at Texas Motor Speedway with a speed of 152.705 mph?

    a. **Carl Edwards**
    b. **Tony Stewart**
    c. **Kurt Busch**
    d. **Jeff Gordon**

495. As of the beginning of the 2012 season, which driver has the most wins in the NASCAR premier series at Watkins Glen International?

    a. **Ricky Rudd**
    b. **Jeff Gordon**
    c. **Tony Stewart**
    d. **Rusty Wallace**

496. As of the beginning of the 2012 season, which current driver is tied with Dale Earnhardt for the most poles in the NASCAR premier series at Watkins Glen International?

    a. Jeff Gordon
    b. Mark Martin
    c. Terry Labonte
    d. Todd Bodine

497. As of the beginning of the 2012 season, which driver holds the NASCAR premier series qualifying record at Watkins Glen International with a speed of 126.421 mph?

    a. Kyle Busch
    b. Jeff Gordon
    c. Mark Martin
    d. Tim Richmond

498. As of the beginning of the 2012 season, which driver holds the NASCAR premier series race record at Watkins Glen International with a speed of 103.030 mph?

    a. Mark Martin
    b. Ernie Irvan
    c. Marcos Ambrose
    d. Marvin Panch

499. Which NASCAR driver performed the Ickey Shuffle in Victory Lane after winning the Daytona 500?

    a. **Dale Earnhardt**
    b. **Darrell Waltrip**
    c. **Jeff Gordon**
    d. **Ryan Newman**

500. How much, on average, does a NASCAR Sprint Cup Series team spend on gas during a race?

    a. **$0**
    b. **$250**
    c. **$500**
    d. **$750**

501. Which driver won the 50th running of the Daytona 500?

    a. **Ryan Newman**
    b. **Jimmie Johnson**
    c. **Dale Earnhardt**
    d. **Matt Kenseth**

502. Which company designs and creates the NASCAR Hall of Fame inductee rings?

    a. **Tiffany & Co.**
    b. **Herff Jones**
    c. **Jostens**
    d. **Balfour**

503. Which NASCAR premier series driver has the most wins in restrictor-plate races in the series?

    a. **Richard Petty**
    b. **Dale Earnhardt**
    c. **Jeff Gordon**
    d. **Jimmie Johnson**

504. The No. 13 race car has only won once in the NASCAR premier series. Which driver is responsible for that victory?

    a. **Johnny Rutherford**
    b. **Buck Baker**
    c. **A.J. Foyt**
    d. **Peck Peckham**

505. The No. 01 race car has only visited Victory Lane once in the NASCAR premier series. Who was behind the steering wheel of the No. 01 race car for that win?

    a. **Mark Martin**
    b. **Joe Nemechek**
    c. **Jason Leffler**
    d. **Paul Goldsmith**

506. Who was the 100th individual driver to win a race in the NASCAR premier series?

    a. **Paul Lewis**
    b. **Mario Andretti**
    c. **Bobby Allison**
    d. **Buddy Baker**

507. Who drove the No. 09 race car to its only victory in the NASCAR premier series?

    a. **Sterling Marlin**
    b. **Buckshot Jones**
    c. **Larry Manning**
    d. **Brad Keselowski**

508. The No. 30 race car has only won once in the NASCAR premier series. Which driver is responsible for the victory?

    a. Speedy Thompson
    b. Dave Marcis
    c. Walter Ballard
    d. Tighe Scott

509. The No. 37 race car has only visited Victory Lane once in the NASCAR premier series. Which driver piloted the race car to the win?

    a. John Andretti
    b. Jeremy Mayfield
    c. Tim Richmond
    d. Bobby Isaac

510. The No. 53 race car has only taken the checkered flag once in the NASCAR premier series. Who was driving when it won?

    a. Bob Burdick
    b. Jimmy Helms
    c. Slick Johnson
    d. Bobby Isaac

511. Who drove the No. 56 race car to its only victory in the NASCAR premier series?

    a. **Martin Truex Jr.**
    b. **LeeRoy Yarbrough**
    c. **Jim Hurtubise**
    d. **Tommy Gale**

512. The No. 58 race car has won only once in the NASCAR premier series. Which driver is responsible for the victory?

    a. **Ricky Craven**
    b. **Johnny Allen**
    c. **Hut Stricklin**
    d. **Johnny Beauchamp**

513. The No. 60 race car has only visited Victory Lane once in the NASCAR premier series? Which driver piloted the No. 60 race car to the win?

    a. **Geoff Bodine**
    b. **Bill Rexford**
    c. **Boris Said**
    d. **Tom Cox**

514. The No. 66 race car has only taken the checkered flag once in the NASCAR premier series. Who was driving when it won?

    a. **Larry Frank**
    b. **Dick Trickle**
    c. **Todd Bodine**
    d. **Jeff Green**

515. Who drove the No. 62 race car to its only victory in the NASCAR premier series?

    a. **Curtis Crider**
    b. **Joe Ruttman**
    c. **Pepper Cunningham**
    d. **Frankie Schneider**

516. The no. 77 race car has only visited Victory Lane once in the NASCAR premier series. Which driver piloted it to the win?

    a. **Chuck Mahoney**
    b. **Joe Lee Johnson**
    c. **Greg Sacks**
    d. **Dave Blaney**

517. The No. 80 race car has won only once in the NASCAR premier series. Which driver is responsible for the victory?

    a. Jim Paschal
    b. Jimmy Horton
    c. E.J. Trivette
    d. Fred Lorenzen

518. The No. 81 race car has taken the checkered flag once in the NASCAR premier series. Who was driving when it won?

    a. Kenny Wallace
    b. J.J. Yeley
    c. Terry Labonte
    d. Danny Graves

519. The No. 86 race car has won once in the NASCAR premier series. Which driver is responsible for the victory?

    a. Tim Flock
    b. Doug Cox
    c. Buck Baker
    d. Tiny Lund

520. Who drove the No. 90 race car to its only victory in the NASCAR premier series?

    a. Jody Ridley
    b. Bill Dennis
    c. Ricky Rudd
    d. Ken Schrader

ANSWER KEY

MULTIPLE CHOICE

1. **B.** The first Daytona 500 was held at Daytona International Speedway on February 22, 1959.

2. **B.** Shorty Rollins won the Rookie of the Year award in 1958, finishing fourth in the final points standings with one victory and 22 top-10 finishes.

3. **A.** Tony Stewart won a NASCAR premier series championship under the previous format in 2002 and then in both 2005 and 2011 under the Chase format.

4. **B.** As of the beginning of the 2012 season, Jeff Gordon had earned 85 trips to Victory Lane in the NASCAR Sprint Cup Series.

5. **D.** Dick Trickle was 56 years, 10 months and 8 days old when he won at Darlington Raceway in September 1998, 2 years, 8 months and 6 days older than the previous record holder, Harry Gant.

6. **C.** Martinsville Speedway hosted its first NASCAR premier series race on September 25, 1949, with Red Byron winning the 105-mile event.

7. **C.** Greg Biffle's hometown is Vancouver, Washington.

8. **B.** While SPEED does not host any NASCAR Sprint Cup Series points events, it did host the 2012 NASCAR Sprint All-Star Race and the 2012 NASCAR Camping World Truck Series season.

9. **A.** On November 24, 1996, in Suzuka, Japan, NASCAR hosted the Thunder Special 100 at the Suzuka Circuit, which Rusty Wallace won. This was the first of three NASCAR exhibition races run in Japan.

10. **B.** The final NASCAR premier series race to allow convertibles was held on May 12, 1962, at Darlington Raceway. Nelson Stacy beat Marvin Panch to the finish line by two car lengths after leading 15 of the 219 laps.

11. **C.** The banking in the corners at Dover International Speedway is currently 24 degrees, while the banking on the frontstretch and backstretch is nine.

12. **D.** Red Byron started six races in 1949, four races in 1950 and five races in 1951, winning the inaugural NASCAR premier series title in 1949.

13. **A.** Linden Airport hosted its only event in the NASCAR premier series on June 13, 1954, with Al Keller winning the 100-mile road course event in a Jaguar.

14. **C.** Bobby Allison led at least one lap in 39 straight NASCAR premier series races between September 6, 1971, and October 22, 1972. Darrell Waltrip and Cale Yarborough are tied for second with 25 consecutive races. Jeff Gordon is the

highest-placing active driver; he is eighth on the all-time list with 19 consecutive races in which he has led at least one lap.

15. D. Although David Pearson was not part of the NASCAR Hall of Fame's inaugural class, he was one of the five inductees enshrined the following year.

16. B. Janet Guthrie had 33 NASCAR premier series starts in five years with five top-10 finishes. Louise Smith is second with 11 starts in four years.

17. A. Marbles are primarily formed by the rubber that burns off the race cars' tires during the race and can sometimes affect cars running over them.

18. C. The Solar Farm facility on the Pocono Raceway grounds, just outside the track, consists of almost 40,000 photovoltaic modules and will produce more than 72 million kilowatt hours of energy over 20 years.

19. C. Mike Skinner started 16th in the inaugural race of the NASCAR Camping World Truck Series. Skinner, driving Richard Childress Racing's No. 3 GM Goodwrench Service Chevrolet, led 30 of the 80 laps to beat Terry Labonte by 0.09 seconds.

20. B. After winning none of the first 26 races of the 2011 NASCAR

Sprint Cup Series season, Tony Stewart won five races in the Chase for the NASCAR Sprint Cup.

21. **D.** Darrell Waltrip has nine pole awards on road courses in the NASCAR premier series. His last pole award on a road course came on June 1, 1986, at Riverside International Raceway in California.

22. **B.** Glenn "Fireball" Roberts led 29 of the 56 laps piloting the No. 22 DePaolo Engineering Ford and finished in front of Curtis Turner and Marvin Panch.

23. **C.** On February 28, 1960, Richard Petty led 18 of 200 laps on the half-mile dirt track to win the 100-mile event at Southern States Fairgrounds (North Carolina), six car lengths in front of Rex White.

24. **B.** In 1953, Lee Petty won the inaugural NASCAR premier series' Most Popular Driver Award. Today the award is given out by the National Motorsports Press Association.

25. **B.** Bill Elliott has won the NASCAR premier series Most Popular Driver Award 16 times (1984–1988, 1991–2000, 2002). Dale Earnhardt Jr. (2003–2011) and Richard Petty (1962, 1964, 1968, 1970, 1974–1978) are tied for second with nine wins.

26. **B.** Charlotte Motor Speedway, the one-and-a-half-mile track in

Concord, North Carolina, owned by Speedway Motorsports, Inc., is found in the heart of NASCAR country and is close to many NASCAR teams' race shops.

27. **C.** The quarter-mile paved track, located in Randleman, North Carolina, hosted three NASCAR premier series events. Jim Paschal (twice) and Richard Petty are the only two drivers in the series to be victorious on the track.

28. **D.** Construction of the NASCAR Hall of Fame began on January 25, 2007. The facility is connected to the Charlotte Convention Center, and has an adjoining 19-story office tower. The NASCAR Hall of Fame officially opened on May 11, 2010.

29. **C.** The No. 61 was retired from competition in the NASCAR Modified Tour.

30. **B.** Richie Evans drove the No. 61 to nine national NASCAR Modified Tour championships, eight of which were consecutive (1973, 1978–1985). He also won an estimated 477 races in the NASCAR Modified Tour.

31. **A.** David Pearson earned the moniker "The Silver Fox" in 1974 for his sly moves on the race track.

32. **C.** Denny Hamlin won on his first trip to the triangular track on

June 11, 2006. He beat Kurt Busch to the checkers by 1.328 seconds. Later that summer, on July 23, 2006, Hamlin once again defeated Kurt Busch, this time by a margin of 1.510 seconds.

33. **D.** Sterling Marlin won his 10th victory in the NASCAR premier series in his 544th start on March 17, 2002, at Darlington Raceway. The victory was his second of the season after winning at Las Vegas Motor Speedway two races earlier.

34. **C.** Matt Kenseth had two seasons (2008 and 2010) between 2002 and 2011 where he did not collect a first-place finish.

35. **D.** Carl Edwards has three victories in the NASCAR Sprint Cup Series at Texas Motor Speedway. Jeff Burton, Denny Hamlin and Matt Kenseth, along with Tony Stewart, each have two wins at the track.

36. **B.** Kentucky Speedway hosted its first NASCAR Sprint Cup Series race on July 9, 2011. Kyle Busch led 125 laps of the 267-lap event and narrowly won the race, beating second-place David Reutimann by just 0.179 seconds.

37. **C.** In the new points system, introduced for the three national series prior to the 2011 season, a race winner could potentially earn a total of 48 points: 43 points for finishing first, 3 points for winning the race, 1 point for leading at least one lap and 1 point for leading the most laps.

38. A. Jeff Gordon has the longest active streak with 20 seasons (1993–2012). He shares that record with David Pearson (1963–1982).

39. D. On September 4, 1950, Darlington Raceway became NASCAR's first paved superspeedway when it hosted the Southern 500, which was won by Johnny Mantz.

40. C. On March 24, 1970, Buddy Baker became the first driver to post a speed faster than 200 mph in a stock car. He achieved this during testing at Talladega Superspeedway.

41. B. According to the *2012 NASCAR Sprint Cup Series Media Guide*, the "modern era" of NASCAR began when the series' schedule was cut from 48 to 31 races.

42. B. The standard weight for the NASCAR Sprint Cup and NASCAR Nationwide Series cars is 3,450 pounds without a driver. The weight for a truck in the NASCAR Camping World Truck Series is 3,400 pounds without a driver.

43. C. Ryan Truex of Mayetta, New Jersey, Martin Truex Jr.'s younger brother, won both the 2009 and 2010 NASCAR K&N Pro Series East championships.

44. D. The greenhouse is the part of the cockpit that is above the bottom of the windshield and windows. Through it, race fans can see the uppermost part of the driver in the cockpit.

45. **A.** The pit crew of the No. 31 Caterpillar Chevrolet, driven by Jeff Burton, captured the title and set an event record time of 22.115 seconds.

46. **C.** South Dakota's Rapid Valley Speedway in Rapid City hosted one race in the NASCAR premier series, while the Louisiana Fairgrounds in Shreveport hosted a single race in 1953 and Maine's Oxford Plains Speedway in Oxford hosted three races between 1966 and 1968. However, Utah has never hosted a NASCAR Sprint Cup Series race.

47. **B.** Idaho, Mississippi and Vermont have never hosted a NASCAR Sprint Cup Series race, but the Oklahoma State Fairgrounds in Oklahoma City hosted one series event in 1956.

48. **C.** Steve Phelps, NASCAR Senior Vice President and Chief Marketing Officer, appeared on an episode of *Undercover Boss* as Kevin Thomas from Vermont.

49. **C.** The new tires that NASCAR teams use during a race are called "stickers" because they usually still have the manufacturer's stickers on them.

50. D. Jimmie Johnson was a varsity water polo player at Granite Hills High School in California.

51. A. Prior to the 2011 NASCAR season, NASCAR officials announced that over-the-wall pit crews would no longer be able to send over a catch can man during pit stops, dropping the number of over-the-wall pit crew members from seven to six. This decision was made because of the new self-ventilating gas cans, put into use at the beginning of the 2011 season.

52. B. The wider a tire's contact patch is, the more track surface the tire is touching, thus providing more grip.

53. D. Dale Earnhardt Jr. has mentioned that if he hadn't become a NASCAR driver he would have been a mechanic for his late father.

54. B. The NASCAR Sprint Cup Series race length at Sonoma is 219 miles. Bristol Motor Speedway and Martinsville Speedway's race lengths are both more than 260 miles.

55. A. The fuel cell in a NASCAR Sprint Cup, NASCAR Nationwide and NASCAR Camping World Truck Series race car or truck has the capacity to hold 18 gallons of Sunoco Green E15.

56. D. The Ryan Newman Foundation published *Pit Road Pets: NASCAR Stars and Their Pets* in 2006 and *Pit Road Pets: The*

Second Lap: NASCAR Stars and Their Pets in 2010. Portions of the book sales go to different animal-friendly causes.

57. **C.** Donnie Allison and Cale Yarborough started fighting in the infield of Daytona International Speedway on the last lap of the Daytona 500. Donnie's brother, Bobby, stopped to assist his younger brother while Richard Petty sped by to capture the victory.

58. **C.** In 1985, Bill Elliott won Winston's Million Dollar Bonus by winning three of the biggest races on the NASCAR premier series schedule – the Daytona 500, Winston 500 and Southern 500. The one big race Elliott did not win that year was the Coca-Cola 600 at Charlotte Motor Speedway.

59. **D.** On October 15, 2000, Dale Earnhardt earned his 76th and final victory in the NASCAR premier series at Talladega Superspeedway by leading 34 of the 188 laps. He beat Kenny Wallace to the finish line by 0.119 seconds.

60. **B.** Cale Yarborough won his only three NASCAR premier series championships in 1976, 1977 and 1978, when he won 9, 9 and 10 races, respectively.

61. **D.** Jack Roush can usually be spotted walking around the garage and pit-road areas during NASCAR Sprint Cup Series race weekends sporting a Panama-style hat.

62. A. Richard Petty has 157 second-place finishes in NASCAR premier series races. David Pearson has 89 and Bobby Allison 87.

63. C. Bill Rexford won the pole for the May 30, 1951, race at Canfield Fairgrounds in Ohio with a speed of 54.233 mph. Rexford would complete only 115 of the 200 laps before wrecking and finishing 21st out of a field of 38 drivers.

64. B. Texas Motor Speedway, the one-and-a-half-mile speedway, in Fort Worth, Texas, is nicknamed "The Great American Speedway."

65. C. *21 Forever: The Story of Stock Car Driver David Pearson*, published in June 1980, was written by Jim Hunter and David Pearson.

66. A. Fred Lorenzen was known by fans and those in the industry as "Golden Boy," "Fearless Freddie" and "Elmhurst Express."

67. A. Marshall Teague drove the "Fabulous Hudson Hornet" in 20 of the 23 NASCAR premier series races he competed in, winning seven of them. Doc Hudson in *Cars* closely resembles the "Fabulous Hudson Hornet."

68. D. Red Byron won two of the eight races in the 1949 NASCAR premier series season while wearing a brace fastened to the clutch to support his leg.

69. B. In 1968, *Sports Illustrated* called Curtis Turner the "Babe Ruth of Stock Car Racing." He was the first NASCAR driver to appear on the cover of the magazine.

70. A. Victory Junction was Adam Petty's dream to offer a safe place for children with chronic medical conditions and serious illnesses to have fun in a camp-style setting. After Petty passed away in 2000, his parents, Kyle and Pattie, along with Paul Newman, spearheaded the project to see to it that Petty's vision for Victory Junction was carried out.

71. C. On December 1, 1963, Wendell Scott led 27 of the 200 laps at Speedway Park in Jacksonville, Florida, to win his only race in the NASCAR premier series. Buck Baker finished second behind Scott.

72. D. Ricky Rudd won three consecutive NASCAR premier series poles at Sonoma from 1990 to 1992. As of the beginning of the 2012 season, Jeff Gordon is the only other driver to put together two consecutive poles at the track, having accomplished this feat twice.

73. A. The members of "The Alabama Gang" included drivers Bobby Allison, Davey Allison, Donnie Allison, David Bonnett, Neil Bonnett, Red Farmer, Jimmy Means and Hut Stricklin, but not Red Byron.

74. **A.** Ricky Rudd had a streak of 788 consecutive race starts in the NASCAR premier series from January 11, 1981, to November 20, 2005. Terry Labonte previously held the record with 655 consecutive race starts from January 14, 1979, to July 23, 2000. Rusty Wallace also passed Labonte's record, starting in 697 consecutive races; however, Wallace consecutive starts streak ended on the same day that Rudd's did.

75. **B.** Carrell Speedway in Gardena, California, hosted a 100-mile event on April 8, 1951. Marshall Teague, driving a Hudson Hornet, beat Johnny Mantz to the checkers in the NASCAR premier series race.

76. **D.** On February 23, 1958, Paul Goldsmith led all 39 laps and beat Curtis Turner to the finish line by five car lengths in the last race held on the Daytona Beach & Road Course.

77. **A.** Herb Thomas won 12 races during the 1953 NASCAR premier series season with wins at Harnett Speedway, North Wilkesboro Speedway, Powell Motor Speedway, Five Flags Speedway, Tri-City Speedway, Monroe County Fairgrounds, Lakewood Speedway, Rapid Valley Speedway, Davenport Speedway, Princess Anne Speedway, Bloomsburg Fairgrounds and Wilson Speedway. Thomas would win 12 races again during the 1954 season and Tim Flock would win 18 races during the 1955 season.

78. C. On May 16, 1971, the first NASCAR premier series race was held with Winston as the new title sponsor. Donnie Allison led 62 of the 188 laps at Talladega Superspeedway, beating his brother, Bobby, to the finish line by six car lengths.

79. C. Eliso Bowie appeared in the July 31, 1955, NASCAR premier series race at Bay Meadows Race Track in San Mateo, California, where he finished 28th out of 34 entrants in the 250-mile race. Charlie Scott appeared in 1 race in the 1956 season, while Wendell Scott appeared in 495 races between 1961 and 1973. Willy T. Ribbs appeared in 3 races in the NASCAR premier series in 1986.

80. A. Frank Mundy was born Franciso Eduardo Menendez in Atlanta, Georgia. Mundy won three NASCAR premier series races in 52 starts.

81. C. Jimmy Florian drove his Euclid Motor Co.–sponsored Ford to victory in the June 25, 1950, NASCAR premier series event at Dayton Speedway (Ohio). He led 40 of the 200 laps and finished ahead of second-place Dick Linder.

82. D. Lella Lombardi (31st), Christine Beckers (37th) and Janet Guthrie (40th) all competed in the 1977 July race at Daytona International Speedway, which Richard Petty won by 17.7 seconds over Darrell Waltrip.

83. C. Herman Beam was black-flagged during one of the qualifying races for the 1960 Daytona 500 – he had forgotten his helmet. He ran eight laps before NASCAR officials noticed.

84. A. Don Oldenberg piloted a Buick convertible to a 10th-place finish at Altamont-Schenectady Fairgrounds in Altamont, New York, on July 29, 1955. This was the first appearance of a convertible in the NASCAR premier series.

85. C. Heavy fog caused the 191-lap race at Riverside International Raceway to be shortened to only 149 laps. Richard Petty beat Bobby Allison by 61.5 seconds. They were the only two drivers on the lead lap.

86. A. On February 28, 1971, Ontario Motor Speedway hosted the 1,000th NASCAR premier series sanctioned race. A.J. Foyt visited Victory Lane after leading 118 of the 200 laps. He won by 8.5 seconds over Buddy Baker.

87. D. On March 23, 2003, Bristol Motor Speedway hosted the NASCAR premier series' 2,000th sanctioned points race. In the race, Kurt Busch beat Matt Kenseth by 0.39 seconds after leading 116 of the 500 laps.

88. C. On March 28, 1954, Dick Rathmann started 26th out of 26 drivers and went on to win the NASCAR premier series event at

Oakland Stadium, beating second-place finisher Marvin Panch.

89. **C.** Ralph Dale Earnhardt was named after his father, Ralph.

90. **B.** Glenn "Fireball" Roberts earned his nickname as a hard-throwing high-school pitcher.

91. **A.** Sam Bass started creating NASCAR-themed art in the early 1980s. He became NASCAR's first officially licensed artist in 1997.

92. **C.** When IndyCar owner Mickey Thompson asked Glenn "Fireball" Roberts if he was interested in driving his car in the 1962 Indy 500, Roberts declined.

93. **A.** NSCRA stood for the National Stock Car Racing Association. The name had to be changed after it was discovered that another racing organization in Georgia already used it.

94. **D.** After NSCRA was dropped, mechanic Red Vogt suggested "NASCAR," which was accepted in a second vote.

95. **B.** Langhorne Speedway, located in Pennsylvania, was a one-mile circular dirt track that hosted 17 NASCAR premier series races between 1949 and 1957 with Herb Thomas and Dick Rathmann each winning three of the events.

96. A. Clifton Burton Marlin gave himself the nickname "Coo Coo" when he was a young child.

97. D. Tony Stewart won the NASCAR Sprint Cup Series championship in 2002 and 2005, both times driving for Joe Gibbs Racing. In 2002, Stewart won 3 of the 36 races and in 2005 won 5 of the 36 races.

98. B. Dale Earnhardt appeared in his debut NASCAR premier series event driving the Ed Negre–owned No. 8 Dodge. In 1976, Earnhardt competed in two NASCAR premier series events, piloting a No. 30 Chevrolet and a No. 77 Chevrolet. He would not get behind the wheel of a No. 2 race car until 1979. He competed in a No. 3 Pontiac in 11 races during the 1981 season. He raced in the No. 15 race car in 1982 and 1983, before going permanently to the No. 3 Chevrolet for the start of the 1984 season.

99. C. 10,000 RPM sponsored Dale Earnhardt's No. 8 Dodge. Earnhardt completed 355 of the 400 laps in the 600-mile event, finishing 22nd of 40 drivers.

100. D. Some past drivers were so superstitious about the denomination of currency that they wouldn't accept a $50 bill from anyone. Dale Earnhardt and Sterling Marlin were just two of the drivers who carried this superstition.

101. A. Richard Petty drove a Ford in 48 of the 50 races during the 1969 NASCAR premier series season, winning ten. Prior to that season, Petty primarily drove Plymouths. After 1969, he primarily drove a Dodge or Pontiac.

102. C. Former NASCAR premier series driver Brett Bodine, who appeared in 480 races during an 18-season career in the series, is now the official pace car driver at NASCAR Sprint Cup Series events.

103. A. Dick Rathmann won the March 28, 1954, NASCAR premier series event at Oakland Stadium while piloting the Ray Erickson–owned No. 3 Hudson. Rathmann only won three events in the No. 3 race car.

104. B. The No. 19 race car is credited with 3 victories in the NASCAR premier series, while the No. 22 has 58, the No. 62 has 1 and the No. 82 has 2.

105. C. Geoff Bodine ran a full NASCAR premier schedule for Rick Hendrick driving the No. 5 Chevrolet in 1984. All-Star Racing and Northwestern Security Life sponsored the race car. Bodine won three races that season.

106. B. Kevin Harvick won by 0.649 seconds over Robert Pressley in the inaugural NASCAR premier series race at Chicagoland

Speedway on July 15, 2001. Harvick led 113 of the 267 laps.

107. **D.** On November 28, 2000, Bill France Jr. passed the role of NASCAR President to Mike Helton, the first non-France family member to hold the position.

108. **C.** Gargoyles sponsored the No. 31 Chevrolet that Dale Earnhardt Jr. drove in the 10th and 17th races of the 1997 NASCAR Nationwide Series season – his 2nd and 3rd races in the series after appearing in one race in 1996.

109. **B.** Tim Flock, driving the Ted Chester–owned No. 91 Oldsmobile, beat second-place finisher John McGinley to the finish line at Pine Grove Speedway in Shippenville, Pennsylvania, which was the track's only series event.

110. **A.** Joe Lee Johnson led 48 of the 400 laps to beat second-place finisher Johnny Beauchamp by more than 4 laps in the inaugural NASCAR premier series event at Charlotte Motor Speedway.

111. **D.** From the 1992 through the 2010 NASCAR Sprint Cup Series season, DuPont was the primary sponsor for Jeff Gordon's No. 24 Chevrolet. At the beginning of their partnership, the race car carried a rainbow paint scheme, thus earning Gordon's pit crew the nickname, "The Rainbow Warriors."

MULTIPLE CHOICE ANSWER KEY

112. B. Rick Mast posted a qualifying speed of 172.414 mph for the inaugural Brickyard 400 at Indianapolis Motor Speedway to capture the pole position over Dale Earnhardt, who had the second-fastest speed during qualifying.

113. B. Jeff Gordon beat Brett Bodine to the finish line by 0.53 seconds to win the inaugural NASCAR premier series event at the Indianapolis Motor Speedway.

114. D. Randy Moss Motorsports scored three wins and three poles, all with Mike Skinner. Prior to Randy Moss joining David Dollar's team, the team was known as Morgan-Dollar Motorsports and they had 13 wins between three different drivers.

115. A. The right- and left-hand turns on road courses picked up the moniker "esses" because they look like the letter S.

116. C. Raymond Parks was the first NASCAR premier series championship winning owner in 1949 with Red Byron, who won two of the eight races that season in only six starts. It was not until 1954 that NASCAR established the official owner's championship points standings.

117. B. Ned Jarrett appeared in 21 races in the 1966 NASCAR premier series season before retiring at the end of the season. Jarrett finished as high as third three times.

118. B. Joey Logano won the 2007 NASCAR K&N Pro Series East championship. The next year Logano made his debuts in all three NASCAR national series, making 1 start in the NASCAR Camping World Truck Series, 3 starts in the NASCAR Sprint Cup Series and 19 starts with one win in the NASCAR Nationwide Series.

119. C. Dale Earnhardt Jr. started the April 2, 2000, race at Texas Motor Speedway fourth, but led 106 of the 334 laps to win his first race in the series by 5.920 seconds over second-place finisher Jeff Burton.

120. D. Elliott Sadler (4th place; Pedigree-sponsored car with Toto), Brendan Gaughan (10th place; Kodak-sponsored car with the Scarecrow), Jeff Gordon (13th place; DuPont-sponsored car with the Cowardly Lion) and Scott Riggs (26th place, Valvoline-sponsored car with the Tin Man) all appeared in the NASCAR premier series race at Kansas Speedway in cars that commemorated the classic movie *The Wizard of Oz.*

121. B. The famous artist, Peter Max, known for his use of bold colors, designed the paint scheme for Dale Earnhardt's No. 3 Goodwrench Chevrolet for the 2000 version of the NASCAR Sprint All-Star Race. Max's use of pinks, yellows and almost every other color of the rainbow was definitely a different look from the standard all-black race car Earnhardt raced in for more than a decade.

122. **A.** The NASCAR Nationwide Series debuted in Mexico at Autodromo Hermanos Rodriguez on March 6, 2005, with Martin Truex Jr. beating Kevin Harvick to the checkers by 6.256 seconds. The series made only three more appearances at the track, visiting for the final time on April 20, 2008.

123. **C.** Dale Earnhardt teamed up with crew chief Dale Inman for 16 races during the 1981 NASCAR premier series season while driving for Rod Osterlund. Although Earnhardt did not win any races while working with Inman, he had 10 top-10 finishes in the 16 starts.

124. **B.** LeeRoy Yarbrough finished his 12-year career with 14 wins in 198 starts in the NASCAR premier series. His first victory came at Savannah Speedway on May 1, 1964, when he beat Marvin Panch by more than one lap.

125. **D.** Seventy-five drivers started the inaugural Southern 500 at Darlington Raceway on September 4, 1950. However, Johnny Mantz was the only driver on the lead lap when he crossed the finish line to win the race, more than nine laps ahead of second-place finisher Glenn "Fireball" Roberts.

126. B. Fonty Flock piloted the Red Devil race car in 32 races and garnered eight wins, while his brother Tim steered the Black Phantom race car to seven victories in 27 races and his other brother, Bob, drove the Gray Ghost to one victory in 13 races in the NASCAR premier series.

127. C. Buck Baker finished ahead of Lee Petty and Bob Welborn to win the only NASCAR premier series race at Gastonia Fairgrounds in North Carolina. Baker, Petty and Welborn were the only drivers in the field of 19 to finish on the lead lap.

128. D. Bobby Allison won three times in the NASCAR premier series behind the wheel of the No. 11 and No. 16 race cars, as well as once in the No. 14 race car. He competed in the No. 29 race car in eight events, but was not victorious. Allison also logged victories in the series in the No. 2, 6, 12, 15, 22, 28 and 88 race cars.

129. C. The track in Hampton, Georgia, was reconfigured in 1997. More grandstand seating was added, which moved the start/finish line and added two doglegs to the frontstretch.

130. B. On June 5, 1983, Ricky Rudd, driving the No. 3 Piedmont Airlines Chevrolet, beat Bill Elliott's No. 9 Melling Oil Pumps Ford to the finish line at Riverside International Raceway

(California) by seven seconds to give Richard Childress Racing its first win in the NASCAR premier series.

131. **A.** Tony Stewart has three victories (2004, 2007 and 2011) at the track that started hosting NASCAR premier series races in 2001. Kevin Harvick is second with two series victories at the track.

132. **D.** Nissan became the 10th participating original-equipment manufacturer in GRAND-AM Road Racing and will support teams in two classes of the Continental Tire Sports Car Challenge.

133. **A.** Matt Kenseth drove the Bill Elliott–owned No. 94 McDonald's Ford to a sixth-place finish in his inaugural start in the NASCAR premier series.

134. **C.** Florida's sportswriters voted Glenn "Fireball" Roberts as the Professional Athlete of the Year in 1958. It was the first time a race car driver from any motorsports league had been named.

135. **B.** In 2010, Triumph Books, a longstanding NASCAR publishing licensee, published the book, *Bill France Jr.: The Man Who Made NASCAR*, commemorating the life of the second President and CEO of NASCAR.

136. A. On June 19, 1949, Jim Roper led 47 of the 197 laps in the NASCAR premier series' inaugural race. Fonty Flock and Red Byron finished second and third, respectively. Glenn Dunaway actually crossed the finish line first, but was disqualified for illegal springs.

137. D. Erwin "Cannonball" Baker was appointed the NASCAR's first National Commissioner at the December 1947 meetings in the Streamline Hotel in Daytona Beach, Florida.

138. C. On February 22, 2004, Matt Kenseth led 259 of the 393 laps in the last NASCAR premier series race at Rockingham Speedway. He beat Kasey Kahne to the checkered flag by 0.010 seconds.

139. D. Mark Martin, behind the wheel of the No. 6 Valvoline/Cummins Ford, drove to the victory in the inaugural race at Las Vegas Motor Speedway. Martin led 82 of the 267 laps and finished 1.605 seconds in front of Jeff Burton.

140. A. Sara Christian was there from the start of NASCAR, appearing in the first NASCAR premier series race on June 19, 1949, at Charlotte Speedway. Christian started 13th and finished 14th after her car overheated.

141. B. Bobby Isaac quit school and went to work at a sawmill at the age of 12 after his parents had both passed away.

142. A. Chip Bolin served as Matt Kenseth's crew chief for the 2008 NASCAR Sprint Cup Series season. That season, Kenseth finished 11th in the final points standings, but did not visit Victory Lane. At the end of the season, Bolin left Kenseth's war wagon to become the head of engineering at Roush Fenway Racing.

143. C. Jeff Gordon decided to unveil his breakdancing skills at the NASCAR After the Lap event on the Thursday night of the 2011 Champion's Week.

144. D. Richard Petty entered 24 of the 31 races during the 1979 NASCAR premier series season behind the wheel of a Chevrolet, winning four times. He appeared in the other seven races that season piloting an Oldsmobile, winning once.

145. B. In the first episode during the second season of *American Pickers*, the pickers showed up to make a deal with Ryan Newman over a Phillips 66 sign.

146. A. When Daytona International Speedway was being built in the 1950s, dirt from the infield was used to create the track's steep banking. The hole that was created as a result of the dirt

removal was filled in with water and named Lake Lloyd after
Joseph Saxton Lloyd, an original member of the speedway
authority.

147. C. Carl Edwards appeared as Eddie Clutch, the owner of a
go-kart track, in an episode of *Kick Buttowski: Suburban Daredevil*.

148. C. Marcos Ambrose is officially from Launceston, Tasmania, in
Australia.

149. A. On July 29, 1961, Bristol Motor Speedway hosted its first
NASCAR premier series race. Jack Smith won by two laps and
22 seconds over Glenn "Fireball" Roberts.

150. A. Jeff Gordon hosted the live comedy show on January 11,
2003. Avril Lavigne was the musical guest.

151. D. Jeff Burton is a huge Duke University basketball fan and has
supported the Duke's Children Hospital for many years.

152. B. Marshall Teague won the NASCAR premier series races at
the Daytona Beach & Road Course on February 11, 1951, and
February 10, 1952. Tim Flock also won the track's races in
back-to-back years on February 27, 1955, and February 26, 1956.

153. D. Former Martinsville Speedway owner, Clay Earles, decided to start awarding the NASCAR premier series race winners Ridgeway grandfather clocks from the Martinsville-based Ridgeway Clocks in 1964. The first clock winner was Fred Lorenzen.

154. **A.** Robby Gordon earned his only pole in the NASCAR premier series by posting a speed of 186.507 mph at Atlanta Motor Speedway for the March 9, 1997, race. Gordon would finish one lap down in 14th place.

155. **B.** Miles the Monster is a concrete mascot that got its name from the track's nickname, "The Monster Mile." A towering statue of Miles sits outside the track's entrance. After each NASCAR Sprint Cup Series race, a replica of the winning race car is placed in Miles's right hand.

156. **C.** Carl Edwards visited Victory Lane nine times during the 2008 NASCAR Sprint Cup Series season to Jimmie Johnson's six trips. However, at the end of the season it was Johnson who claimed the championship by 69 points over Edwards.

157. **C.** Tony Stewart, Carl Edwards, Joey Logano and Brian Vickers all appeared on an episode of the A&E show, *The Glades*. The episode, in which the drivers played themselves, aired on June 26, 2011.

158. C. The NASCAR news talk show, *Inside NASCAR*, airs on SHOWTIME. The original cast was Chris Myers, Brad Daugherty, Randy Pemberton and Michael Waltrip.

159. B. Former driver Kyle Petty, who had eight victories in his NASCAR premier series career, joined the *Inside NASCAR* cast prior to beginning of the 2011 season.

160. B. Indianapolis Motor Speedway has, by far, the largest grandstand capacity at more than 250,000. Bristol Motor Speedway has the second most with a grandstand capacity of 160,000.

161. D. Dale Earnhardt was actually leading Bill Elliott when the latter forced Earnhardt down into the grass. Since Earnhardt was already ahead and never gave up the lead to Elliott, Earnhardt never really "passed" Bill Elliott. Therefore, one of Earnhardt's most famous moments on track is misnamed.

162. C. The famous pass-that-wasn't-an-actual-pass took place in the 1987 version of what is now the NASCAR Sprint All-Star Race.

163. D. Victory Junction is scheduled to open its second facility near Kansas Speedway in Kansas City, Kansas. The original camp is located in Randleman, North Carolina.

164. B. Jeff Gordon has won at every track that currently hosts a

MULTIPLE CHOICE ANSWER KEY

NASCAR Sprint Cup Series event except Homestead-Miami Speedway and Kentucky Speedway.

165. A. David Ragan, who won his first NASCAR Sprint Cup Series race in 2011 at Daytona International Speedway, joined Front Row Motorsports to pilot the No. 34 Ford. Jay Guy would serve as the team's crew chief.

166. C. David Pearson won 6 races in 1972, 11 in 1973, 7 in 1974, 3 in 1975, 10 in 1976, 2 in 1977 and 4 in 1978.

167. C. NASCAR officials allowed slightly larger holes (57/64-inch, a 1/64-inch increase over the previous size) in the restrictor plate for the October 2011 NASCAR Sprint Cup Series race at Talladega Superspeedway, providing the race cars with up to 10 more horsepower.

168. A. First Lady Michelle Obama and Dr. Jill Biden attended the 2011 Ford Championship Weekend at Homestead-Miami Speedway as Grand Marshals for the Ford 400, which was the final race in the NASCAR Sprint Cup Series season.

169. D. Reba McEntire hosted the 2011 NASCAR Sprint Cup Series Awards Ceremony at the Wynn Las Vegas on December 2.

170. B. After racing six seasons and winning 10 races in the NASCAR

Sprint Cup Series for Penske Racing, Kurt Busch joined Phoenix Racing and drove the No. 51 Chevrolet full-time in 2012.

171. C. Although Jeff Gordon was born in California, he grew up in Pittsboro, Indiana, after his family moved there when he was young.

172. A. Ryan Newman earned the nickname "Rocket Man" in 2003 after winning a series-high 11 poles in the NASCAR premier series.

173. C. Rick Hendrick fielded his first race car in the 1984 Daytona 500 with driver Geoff Bodine behind the wheel of the No. 5 All-Star Racing Chevrolet. Bodine finished eighth in the race won by Cale Yarborough.

174. B. On June 27, 1965, Cale Yarborough earned his first win in the NASCAR premier series at Valdosta 75 Speedway in Georgia, leading just 18 of the 200 laps and winning by more than three laps over second-place finisher J.T. Putney. It was Yarborough's only win in the series in 1965, but the first of 83 in his career.

175. C. Trenton Speedway, which hosted its first race in the NASCAR premier series on May 30, 1958, and its last race on July 16, 1972, was shaped like a kidney.

MULTIPLE CHOICE ANSWER KEY

176. **D.** On September 3, 1962, Clint Eastwood attended the Southern 500 at Darlington Raceway in South Carolina as the Grand Marshal. Larry Frank won the race by five seconds over Junior Johnson.

177. **B.** The headquarters for Eutechnyx, which developed the video game *NASCAR: The Game 2011*, is located in Newcastle, England. The game was released in March 2011.

178. **A.** Lee Petty led 29 of the 100 laps to win the only NASCAR premier series race ever at Canadian National Exhibition Speedway in Toronto. Cotton Owens came in second and Rex White led the other 71 laps, finishing seventh.

179. **B.** Buddy Shuman won the only NASCAR premier series race ever to take place at Stamford Park in Niagara Falls, Ontario. He drove the No. 89 Hudson to a victory over second-place finisher Herb Thomas.

180. **D.** Buck Baker led 60 of the 200 laps in the only NASCAR premier series race held at Chisholm Speedway in Alabama. Baker beat Ralph Moody to the finish line in the September 9, 1956, race.

181. **B.** On August 3, 1960, Ned Jarrett, behind the steering wheel of the No. 11 Courtesy Ford, beat Richard Petty to the finish line by more than two laps in the only NASCAR

premier series race ever held at Dixie Speedway in Alabama.

182. C. On August 8, 1962, Richard Petty drove the No. 43 Plymouth to a victory over Bob Welborn by more than a lap in the only NASCAR premier series ever race held at Huntsville Speedway in Alabama.

183. A. On May 15, 1955, Danny Letner drove the No. 6 Oldsmobile to a victory over second-place finisher Allen Adkins in the only NASCAR premier series race ever held at Tucson Rodeo Grounds in Arizona.

184. A. On June 22, 1957, Bill Amick drove the No. 97 Ford to a victory over Lloyd Dane. Amick won by more than one lap in the only NASCAR premier series ever race held at Capitol Speedway in California.

185. A. On June 3, 1956, Herb Thomas drove the No. 300B Chrysler to a victory over second-place finisher Harold Hardesty in the only NASCAR premier series race ever held at Merced Fairgrounds in California.

186. D. On September 15, 1957, Marvin Porter drove the No. 12 Ford to a victory over second-place finisher Eddie Pagan in the only NASCAR premier series race ever held at Santa Clara Fairgrounds in California.

187. B. On June 14, 1953, Herb Thomas drove the No. 92 Hudson to a victory over second-place finisher Dick Rathmann in the only NASCAR premier series race ever held at Five Flags Speedway in Florida.

188. C. On November 11, 1962, Richard Petty drove the No. 43 Plymouth to a one-car-length victory over Jim Paschal in the only NASCAR premier series race ever held at Golden Gate Speedway in Florida.

189. A. On November 17, 1963, Glenn "Fireball" Roberts drove the No. 22 Ford to a victory over Dave MacDonald, winning by one lap and 28 seconds in the only NASCAR premier series race ever held at Augusta International Raceway in Georgia.

190. D. On June 10, 1951, Tim Flock drove the No. 91 Black Phantom Oldsmobile to a victory over second-place finisher Gober Sosebee in the only NASCAR premier series race ever held at Columbus Speedway in Georgia.

191. D. On June 1, 1952, Gober Sosebee drove the No. 51 Chrysler to a 22-second victory over Tommy Moon in the only NASCAR premier series race ever held at Hayloft Speedway in Georgia.

192. B. On August 2, 1953, Herb Thomas drove the No. 92 Fabulous Hudson to a victory over second-place finisher Buck

Baker in the only NASCAR premier series race ever held at Davenport Speedway in Iowa.

193. A. On October 15, 1950, Lloyd Moore drove the No. 59 Mercury to a victory over second-place finisher Bucky Sager in the only NASCAR premier series race ever held at Funks Speedway in Indiana.

194. A. On August 29, 1954, Lee Petty drove the No. 42 Chrysler to a victory over second-place finisher Hershel McGriff in the only NASCAR premier series race ever held at Corbin Speedway in Kentucky.

195. C. On June 7, 1953, Lee Petty drove the No. 42 Dodge to a victory over second-place finisher Dick Rathmann in the only NASCAR premier series race ever held at Louisiana Fairgrounds.

196. A. Norwood Arena, which hosted its only NASCAR premier series event on June 17, 1961, is located in Norwood, Massachusetts.

197. D. Tim Flock drove the No. 91 Hudson to Victory Lane at Monroe Speedway in Michigan on July 6, 1952, beating Herb Thomas to the finish line.

198. B. On March 8, 1953, Herb Thomas drove the No. 92 Fabulous Hudson to a victory over second-place finisher Dick Rathmann in the only NASCAR premier series race ever held at Harnett Speedway in North Carolina.

199. D. On July 12, 1958, Jim Paschal drove the No. 49 Chevrolet to a victory over second-place finisher Cotton Owens in the only NASCAR premier series race ever held at McCormick Field in North Carolina.

200. C. Richard Petty won the Daytona 500 a record seven times: 1964, 1966, 1971, 1973, 1974, 1979 and 1981.

201. A. On October 5, 1958, Lee Petty drove the No. 42 Oldsmobile to a victory over second-place finisher Buck Baker in the only NASCAR premier series race ever held at Salisbury Super Speedway in North Carolina.

202. C. Star Lite Speedway hosted its only NASCAR premier series race ever on May 13, 1966, with Darel Dieringer winning by more than eight laps over Clyde Lynn. It is located in Monroe, North Carolina.

203. B. On July 26, 1953, Dick Rathmann drove the No. 120 Hudson to a victory over the second-place finisher Herb Thomas in the only NASCAR premier series race ever held at Lincoln City Fairgrounds in Nebraska.

204. **A.** On July 26, 1958, Jim Reed drove the No. 7 Chevrolet to a victory over second-place finisher Rex White.

205. **D.** On October 16, 1955, Norm Nelson drove the No. 299 Mercury Outboards Chrysler to a victory over second-place finisher Bill Hyde in the only NASCAR premier series race ever held at Las Vegas Park Speedway in Nevada.

206. **D.** Airborne Speedway, which hosted its only NASCAR premier series race on June 19, 1955, with Lee Petty beating runner-up Buck Baker, is located in Plattsburg, New York.

207. **B.** Jim Reed drove the No. 7 Ford to Victory Lane at Buffalo Civic Stadium in New York on July 19, 1958, beating Cotton Owens to the finish line.

208. **C.** On July 17, 1960, Rex White drove the No. 4 Piedmont/ Friendly Chevrolet to a victory over runner-up Richard Petty in the only NASCAR premier series race ever held at Montgomery Air Base in New York.

209. **A.** On July 16, 1958, Shorty Rollins drove the No. 99 Ford to a victory over runner-up Bob Duell in the only NASCAR premier series race ever held at State Line Speedway in New York.

210. A. On August 4, 1957, Parnelli Jones drove the No. 11 Ford to a victory over second-place finisher Lloyd Dane in the only NASCAR premier series race ever held at Kitsap County Airport in Washington.

211. D. On July 4, 1952, Tim Flock drove the No. 91 Hudson to a victory over runner-up Herb Thomas in the only NASCAR premier series race ever held at Wine Creek Race Track in New York.

212. B. On August 23, 1953, Herb Thomas drove the No. 92 Fabulous Hudson to a victory over second-place finisher Fonty Flock in the only NASCAR premier series race ever held at Princess Anne Speedway in Virginia.

213. C. On May 24, 1953, Herb Thomas drove the No. 92 Fabulous Hudson to a victory over runner-up Dick Rathmann in the only NASCAR premier series race ever held at Powell Motor Speedway in Ohio.

214. A. On May 23, 1954, Lee Petty drove the No. 42 Chrysler to a victory over second-place finisher Buck Baker in the only NASCAR premier series race ever held at Sharon Speedway in Ohio.

215. D. Jim Paschal drove the No. 75 C U Later Alligator Mercury to

Victory Lane at Oklahoma State Fairgrounds in Oklahoma on August 3, 1956, beating Ralph Moody to the finish line by a quarter of a lap.

216. **C.** On October 3, 1953, Herb Thomas drove the No. 92 Fabulous Hudson to a victory over runner-up Dick Rathmann in the only NASCAR premier series race ever held at Bloomsburg Fairgrounds in Pennsylvania.

217. **B.** On June 12, 1958, Junior Johnson drove the No. 11 Ford to a victory over second-place finisher Lee Petty in the only NASCAR premier series race ever held at New Bradford Speedway in Pennsylvania.

218. **D.** Pine Grove Speedway, which hosted its only NASCAR premier series race on October 14, 1951, is located in Shippenville, Pennsylvania.

219. **C.** Herb Thomas drove the No. 92 Hudson to Victory Lane at Williams Grove Speedway in Pennsylvania on June 27, 1954, beating Dick Rathmann to the finish line by four car lengths.

220. **A**. On September 15, 1960, Ned Jarrett drove the No. 11 Courtesy Ford to a victory over second-place finisher David Pearson in the only NASCAR premier series race ever held at Gamecock Speedway in South Carolina.

221. A. Only 13 drivers started the September 15, 1960, NASCAR premier series race at Gamecock Speedway. Ten of the drivers were running at the end of the race with only two drivers completing all 200 laps.

222. B. On June 23, 1971, Bobby Allison drove the No. 12 Dodge to a victory over second-place finisher James Hylton by more than two laps in the only NASCAR premier series race ever held at Meyer Speedway in Texas.

223. D. On October 12, 1957, Glenn "Fireball" Roberts drove the No. 22 Ford to a victory over runner-up Buck Baker in the only NASCAR premier series race ever held at Newberry Speedway in South Carolina.

224. A. On July 22, 1953, Herb Thomas drove the No. 92 Fabulous Hudson to a victory over second-place finisher Dick Rathmann in the only NASCAR premier series race held at Rapid Valley Speedway in South Dakota.

225. C. On June 23, 1961, Buck Baker drove the No. 86 Chrysler to a victory over runner-up Jack Smith in the only NASCAR premier series race ever held at Hartsville Speedway in South Carolina.

226. A. With finishes of 4th, 8th, 3rd, 5th, 3rd, 11th, 9th, 2nd, 2nd and 2nd in the final 10 races of the 2011 NASCAR Sprint Cup

Series season, Carl Edwards had an average finishing position of 4.9 in those races.

227. A. On September 18, 1949, Jack White earned his only victory in the NASCAR premier series. This occurred at Hamburg Speedway in New York. White beat Ray Erickson to the finish line.

228. C. Sara Christian placed 14th in the August 27, 1950, NASCAR premier series race at Hamburg Speedway. Ann Chester and Louise Smith placed 21st and 22nd, respectively.

229. C. On February 25, 1966, Earl Balmer earned his only victory in the NASCAR premier series. The race was held at Daytona International Speedway in Florida. Balmer beat Jim Hurtubise to the finish line by four car lengths.

230. D. On November 3, 2002, Johnny Benson earned his only victory in the NASCAR premier series. This happened at Rockingham Speedway in North Carolina. Benson beat Mark Martin to the finish line by 0.261 seconds.

231. B. On April 22, 1990, Brett Bodine earned his only victory in the NASCAR premier series. It occurred at North Wilkesboro Speedway in North Carolina. Bodine beat Darrell Waltrip to the finish line by 0.95 seconds.

232. **B.** Pete Allen won the 1953 NASCAR Speedway Division, the second and final year the division existed.

233. **C.** On June 16, 1962, Johnny Allen earned his only victory in the NASCAR premier series. This occurred at Bowman Gray Stadium in Winston-Salem, North Carolina. Allen beat Rex White to the finish line by six inches.

234. **A.** On August 12, 1973, Dick Brooks earned his only victory in the NASCAR premier series. The race was run at Talladega Superspeedway in Alabama. Brooks beat Buddy Baker to the finish line by 7.2 seconds.

235. **D.** On March 26, 1961, Bob Burdick earned his only victory in the NASCAR premier series. The race was run at Atlanta Motor Speedway in Hampton, Georgia. Burdick captured the checkered flag under caution.

236. **A.** On October 14, 1951, Marvin Burke earned his only victory in the NASCAR premier series. The race was run at Oakland Stadium in California. Burke beat Robert Caswell to the finish line.

237. **C.** On October 12, 1951, Neil Cole earned his only victory in the NASCAR premier series. The race was run at Thompson Speedway in Connecticut. Cole beat Jim Reed to the finish line.

238. B. On September 11, 1960, Jim Cook earned his only victory in the NASCAR premier series. The race was run at California State Fairgrounds in Sacramento, California. Cook beat Scotty Cain to the finish line.

239. A. On January 21, 1973, Mark Donohue earned his only victory in the NASCAR premier series. The race was run at Riverside International Raceway in California. Donohue beat Bobby Allison to the finish line by more than one lap.

240. C. On September 28, 1958, Joe Eubanks earned his only victory in the NASCAR premier series. The race was run at Occoneechee Speedway in Hillsboro, North Carolina. Eubanks beat Doug Cox to the finish line by half a lap.

241. A. On June 30, 1951, Lou Figaro earned his only victory in the NASCAR premier series. This occurred at Carrell Speedway in Gardena, California. Figaro beat Chuck Meekins to the finish line by 100 yards.

242. D. On May 30, 1954, John Soares earned his only victory in the NASCAR premier series. The race was run at Carrell Speedway in Gardena, California. Soares beat Lloyd Dane to the finish line.

243. C. On September 3, 1962, Larry Frank earned his only victory in the NASCAR premier series. The race was run at Darlington

Raceway in South Carolina. Frank beat Junior Johnson to the finish line by five seconds.

244. **C.** On September 8, 1957, Danny Graves earned his only victory in the NASCAR premier series. The race was run at California State Fairgrounds in Sacramento, California. Graves beat Marvin Porter to the finish line.

245. **D.** On August 26, 1956, Royce Haggerty earned his only victory in the NASCAR premier series. The win came at Portland Speedway in Oregon. Haggerty beat Clyde Palmer to the finish line.

246. **A.** On July 27, 1986, Bobby Hillin Jr. earned his only victory in the NASCAR premier series. The race was run at Talladega Superspeedway in Alabama. Hillin beat Tim Richmond to the finish line by three car lengths.

247. **A.** On March 27, 1966, Jim Hurtubise earned his only victory in the NASCAR premier series. The race was run at Atlanta Motor Speedway in Hampton, Georgia. Hurtubise beat Fred Lorenzen to the finish line by more than one lap.

248. **B.** On June 24, 1956, John Kieper earned his only victory in the NASCAR premier series. The race was held at Portland Speedway in Oregon. Kieper beat second-place Clyde Palmer to the finish line.

249. **D.** On February 5, 1950, Harold Kite earned his only victory in the NASCAR premier series. The race was run at the Daytona Beach & Road Course in Florida. Kite beat Red Byron to the finish line by 53 seconds.

250. **C.** After working as the crew chief and winning the NASCAR Sprint Cup Series championship with the No. 14 team, Darian Grubb left Stewart-Haas Racing to join up with Denny Hamlin and the No. 11 FedEx Toyota team at Joe Gibbs Racing for the 2012 season.

251. **B.** On July 28, 1966, Paul Lewis earned his only victory in the NASCAR premier series. The race was run at Smokey Mountain Raceway in Maryville, Tennessee. Lewis beat David Pearson to the finish line by two seconds.

252. **B.** On September 4, 1950, Johnny Mantz earned his only victory in the NASCAR premier series. The race was held at Darlington Raceway in South Carolina. Mantz beat Glenn "Fireball" Roberts to the finish line by more than nine laps.

253. **C.** Sam McQuagg beat Darel Dieringer to the finish line by one minute and six seconds at Daytona International Speedway in Florida, on July 4, 1966.

254. **A.** On March 27, 1988, Lake Speed earned his only victory in

MULTIPLE CHOICE ANSWER KEY

the NASCAR premier series. The race was held at Darlington Raceway in South Carolina. Speed beat Alan Kulwicki to the finish line by 18.8 seconds.

255. **C.** On November 20, 1955, Chuck Stevenson earned his only victory in the NASCAR premier series. The race was held at Willow Springs Speedway in Lancaster, California. Stevenson beat Marvin Panch to the finish line by 500 feet.

256. **D.** On November 20, 2000, Jerry Nadeau earned his only victory in the NASCAR premier series. The race was run at Atlanta Motor Speedway in Hampton, Georgia. Nadeau beat Dale Earnhardt to the finish line by 1.338 seconds.

257. **C.** On November 16, 1952, Donald Thomas earned his only victory in the NASCAR premier series. The race was run at Lakewood Speedway in Atlanta, Georgia. Thomas beat second-place Lee Petty to the finish line.

258. **D.** On November 11, 1951, Bill Norton earned his only victory in the NASCAR premier series. The race was run at Carrell Speedway in Gardena, California. Norton beat Dick Meyer to the finish line.

259. **B.** On May 1, 1988, Phil Parsons earned his only victory in the NASCAR premier series. The race was run at Talladega

M U L T I P L E C H O I C E A N S W E R K E Y

Superspeedway in Alabama. Parsons beat Bobby Allison to the finish line by 0.21 seconds.

260. **A.** On April 5, 1953, Dick Passwater earned his only victory in the NASCAR premier series. The race was run at Charlotte Speedway in North Carolina. Passwater beat Gober Sosebee to the finish line by a quarter of a lap.

261. **B.** On August 6, 1978, Lennie Pond earned his only victory in the NASCAR premier series. The race was run at Talladega Superspeedway in Alabama. Pond beat Donnie Allison to the finish line by a foot.

262. **D.** On August 12, 1951, Tommy Thompson earned his only victory in the NASCAR premier series. The race was run at Michigan State Fairgrounds in Detroit, Michigan. Thompson beat Joe Eubanks to the finish line by 37 seconds.

263. **A.** On May 30, 1950, Bill Rexford earned his only victory in the NASCAR premier series. The race was run at Canfield Fairgrounds in Ohio. Rexford beat Glenn Dunaway to the finish line.

264. **A.** On May 17, 1981, Jody Ridley earned his only victory in the NASCAR premier series. The race was run at Dover International Speedway in Delaware. Ridley beat Bobby Allison to the finish line by 22 seconds.

265. C. On June 3, 2007, Martin Truex Jr. earned his only victory in the NASCAR premier series. The race was run at Dover International Speedway in Delaware. Truex beat Ryan Newman to the finish line by 7.355 seconds.

266. C. Art Watts was born on November 25, 1917, making him 39 years old on April 28, 1957, when he earned his only victory in the NASCAR premier series.

267. B. On September 29, 1974, Earl Ross earned his only victory in the NASCAR premier series. The race was run at Martinsville Speedway in Virginia. Ross beat Buddy Baker to the finish line by more than one lap.

268. A. On April 3, 1960, John Rostek earned his only victory in the NASCAR premier series. The race was run at Arizona State Fairgrounds in Phoenix, Arizona. Rostek beat second-place Mel Larson to the finish line.

269. D. On July 4, 1985, Greg Sacks earned his only victory in the NASCAR premier series. The race was run at Daytona International Speedway in Florida. Sacks beat Bill Elliott to the finish line by 23.5 seconds.

270. A. On August 2, 1981, Ron Bouchard earned his only victory in the NASCAR premier series. The race was run at Talladega

Superspeedway in Alabama. Bouchard beat Darrell Waltrip to the finish line by two feet.

271. **B.** On September 24, 1950, Leon Sales earned his only victory in the NASCAR premier series. The race was run at North Wilkesboro Speedway in North Carolina. Sales beat second-place Jack Smith to the finish line.

272. **C.** On April 25, 1958, Frankie Schneider earned his only victory in the NASCAR premier series. The race was run at Old Dominion Speedway in Manassas, Virginia. Schneider beat Jack Smith to the finish line.

273. **C.** On October 28, 1951, Danny Weinberg earned his only victory in the NASCAR premier series. The race was run at Marchbanks Speedway in Hanford, California. Weinberg beat Marvin Panch to the finish line.

274. **D.** Harold Brasington returned from the 1933 Indianapolis 500 with the idea of building a superspeedway in Darlington, South Carolina. Many locals believed Brasington's idea was crazy, but in 1949 he started working toward building Darlington Raceway.

275. **B.** On February 27, 2012, Matt Kenseth held off Dale Earnhardt Jr. to win the 2012 Daytona 500. The race had been delayed for

more than 36 hours because of weather and included a 2-hour plus red-flag stop that caused the finish to be delayed until early Tuesday morning.

276. **A.** The NASCAR Sprint Cup Series Awards Ceremony was held in Daytona Beach, Florida, until 1981 when it moved to the Waldorf-Astoria Hotel in New York City. Then in 2009, the ceremony moved to the Wynn Las Vegas in Las Vegas, Nevada.

277. **C.** Even though Sunoco has longstanding relationships within the NASCAR industry, it wasn't until 2004 that Sunoco became the Official Fuel of the top-3 NASCAR series.

278. **B.** In 2000, Dale Earnhardt Jr. became the first rookie in the NASCAR premier series to win the NASCAR Sprint All-Star Race. That year, Earnhardt fell 42 points shy of winning Rookie of the Year, which went to Matt Kenseth.

279. **C.** On March 5, 2011, Danica Patrick placed fourth in the NASCAR Nationwide Series race at Las Vegas Motor Speedway. This broke the previous record for the best finish by a female driver in the top-3 series which was previously held by Sara Christian, who finished fifth in the October 2, 1949, race at Heidelberg Raceway in Pittsburgh, Pennsylvania.

280. A. Ned Jarrett had 13 wins and 42 top-5 finishes in the 1965 NASCAR premier series on his way to his second championship. David Pearson had 11 wins and 42 top-5 finishes in the 1969 NASCAR premier series on his way to his third championship.

281. C. In 2011, Chevrolet earned their 35th Manufacturers Championship in the NASCAR premier series and their 31st since 1972.

282. B. The Ford Fusion has been the model of choice in the NASCAR premier series since 2006. Past Ford models include the Taurus, Thunderbird, Torino, Galaxie and Fairlane.

283. D. Jayne Mansfield was the Grand Marshal for the March 10, 1963, NASCAR premier series race at the Hillsboro, North Carolina, track. Junior Johnson won the race and received a kiss from Mansfield.

284. B. In August 2011, Chrissy Wallace, daughter of NASCAR driver Mike Wallace, became the first female to win the ASA Late Model championship at Lebanon I-44 Speedway. She has appeared in seven NASCAR Camping World Truck Series races and two NASCAR Nationwide Series races.

285. C. According to the minutes from the meetings, there were 36 people in attendance over the four days. In attendance were

MULTIPLE CHOICE ANSWER KEY

drivers, car owners, mechanics, promoters, businessmen, journalists and other race-sanctioning executives.

286. A. Driver Lee Petty was not in attendance at the 1947 meetings, but drivers Chuck DiNatale, Joe Ross, Sammy Packard, Lucky Sauer, Fred Dagavar, Marshall Teague, Red Byron, Fonty Flock, Frank Mundy and Buddy Shuman were there.

287. B. In 1948, prior to the inaugural season of what is now known as the NASCAR Sprint Cup Series, Raymond Parks fielded more than one car in NASCAR-sanctioned action.

288. D. Red Vogt was presented with the first NASCAR membership card by Bill France, in part for coming up with the sport's name.

289. A. In 1955, Carl Kiekhaefer outfitted his pit crews in uniforms advertising his company, Mercury Marine, which sold outboard motors.

290. C. In 1951, Marshall Teague competed in the NASCAR premier series driving a Hudson Hornet with support from the manufacturer's executives.

291. A. On March 8, 1936, Bill France drove a 1935 Ford coupe in a race on a 3.2-mile track in Daytona Beach that utilized the beach and part of State Road A1A. Milt Marion won the race, with France finishing fifth out of 27.

292. **C.** Richard Petty won NASCAR premier series championships in 1964, 1967, 1971, 1972, 1974, 1975 and 1979. In 1969, Petty finished second, 357 points behind champion David Pearson.

293. **D.** Roof flaps were first introduced in 1994 to help prevent race cars from going airborne during an on-track accident.

294. **D.** Lexan is the shatterproof material manufactured by General Electric that is used for windshields and windows in NASCAR race cars and trucks. However, Lexan does scratch easily.

295. **C.** On April 29, 1982, Benny Parsons became the first driver in NASCAR history to record a qualifying lap over 200 mph. Parsons posted a qualifying speed of 200.176 mph at Talladega Superspeedway.

296. **D.** Richard Petty won six NASCAR premier series races behind the steering wheel of the No. 41 race car, two races in the No. 42 and 192 races in the No. 43. Petty never drove the No. 44, although his brother, Maurice, appeared in the No. 44 once, at Bowman Gray Stadium in 1961.

297. C. Bobby Allison won the 1983 NASCAR premier series championship shortly before his 46th birthday, beating Lee Petty by a couple of months.

298. B. In 1986, Tim Richmond finished third in the final points standings in the NASCAR premier series on the strength of seven victories and 13 top-5 finishes. His next highest finish in the series' final points standings was 10th place in 1983.

299. C. On February 13, 1982, Dale Earnhardt won the first race in the NASCAR Nationwide Series at Daytona International Speedway, competing in the No. 15 Wrangler Jeans Pontiac.

300. D. Kyle Busch won 10 races during the 2008 NASCAR Nationwide Series, but finished sixth in the series final points standings. Clint Bowyer won the championship that year after only winning 1 race. The difference was that Bowyer started all 35 races that season, while Busch only started 30. Busch went on to win the 2009 NASCAR Nationwide Series championship.

301. A. On August 4, 1974, Richard Petty led 152 of 192 laps to capture the victory at the inaugural NASCAR premier series race at Pocono Raceway. He beat Buddy Baker to the finish line by 18.8 seconds.

302. B. On May 30, 1982, Neil Bonnett led 67 laps to win the Coca-Cola 600 at Charlotte Motor Speedway. The next year, on May 29, 1983, Bonnett again visited Victory Lane in the race after leading 69 laps.

303. B. Red Vogt served as Red Byron's crew chief in 1949 on their way to two wins and the inaugural championship in what would become later known as the NASCAR Sprint Cup Series.

304. C. On November 6, 1988, Alan Kulwicki led 41 laps to beat Terry Labonte by 18.5 seconds in the inaugural NASCAR premier series race at Phoenix International Raceway.

305. C. As of the beginning of the 2012 season, Ford has 10 total victories at Texas Motor Speedway in the NASCAR premier series. Chevrolet is second most with 7.

306. D. David Pearson has 10 career victories in the NASCAR premier series at Darlington Raceway, one more than Dale Earnhardt.

307. D. By the time Morgan Shepherd appeared in the 2011 NASCAR Nationwide Series finale at Homestead-Miami Speedway on November 19, 2011, he had already celebrated his 70th birthday.

MULTIPLE CHOICE ANSWER KEY

308. B. Bill Elliott is scheduled to try to qualify the No. 50 Walmart Chevrolet for the 2012 NASCAR Sprint Cup Series July race at Daytona International Speedway in celebration of the retail giant's 50th anniversary.

309. A. On July 10, 2005, David Stremme drove the No. 39 Navy "Accelerate Your Life" Dodge to a 16th-place finish in his first NASCAR premier series race at Chigacoland Speedway.

310. C. Ron Hornaday Jr. has won four championships in the NASCAR Camping World Truck Series (1996, 1998, 2007 and 2009). Jack Sprague is second with three championships in the series.

311. A. Ryan Newman graduated from Purdue University in West Lafayette, Indiana, in August 2001, with a bachelor's degree in Vehicle Structure Engineering.

312. C. Brendan Gaughan played for the Georgetown University Hoyas basketball team from 1993 to 1997. During his time with the team they won two Big East championships and made it to the Elite Eight in the NCAA Basketball Tournament once.

313. B. Michael Annett, who drives the No. 43 Pilot Travel Centers/ Flying J Ford in the 2012 NASCAR Nationwide Series season, played hockey for the Waterloo Black Hawks in the United States Hockey League. He won the Most Improved Player award for his team in 2004 and earned a Clark Cup championship.

314. A. Bill Rexford won the 1950 NASCAR premier series championship at 23 years old, the youngest champion in the series.

315. D. One of the reasons Dale Earnhardt might have been such a great race car driver is because it was believed that he could actually see the air move over his car.

316. C. On May 28, 1995, Bobby Labonte posted a race speed record of 151.952 mph for the 600-mile race in the NASCAR premier series at Charlotte Motor Speedway. He beat Terry Labonte, his older brother, by 6.28 seconds for his first victory in the series.

317. A. In 1969, Bobby Isaac set the NASCAR premier series record with 20 poles in one season. Eleven of the poles led to victories. In addition, Isaac scored six additional wins that season.

318. C. Richard Petty has 61 wins from the pole in the NASCAR premier series. David Pearson is second with 37.

319. A. As of the beginning of the 2012 season, Jeff Gordon has the most victories on superspeedways two miles or longer in the NASCAR premier series with 30. Richard Petty is second with 27.

320. **C.** Richard Petty had earned 148 victories on tracks a mile long or less in NASCAR premier series competition. David Pearson is second with 56.

321. **D.** On August 18, 1991, Dale Jarrett won the NASCAR premier series event at Michigan International Speedway, which was his first, in the No. 21 Citgo Ford owned by the Wood Brothers. He would finish the season 17th in the final points standings.

322. **B.** Ralph Stark owned the No. 40 Chevrolet that Bobby Allison drove in the four races in which he competed in 1961. His best finish that year was a 20th at Daytona International Speedway.

323. **C.** On March 20, 2005, Carl Edwards drove his No. 99 Scotts Ford to victory over Jimmie Johnson for his first victory in the NASCAR premier series. Edwards also won one race that year in a race car sponsored by Stonebridge Life Insurance and two races in a race car sponsored by Office Depot.

324. **A.** Curtis Turner won four races during the 1950 NASCAR premier series season. Dick Linder finished with three and Bill Rexford, the 1950 NASCAR premier series champion, only had one victory, which came at Canfield Fairgrounds in Ohio.

325. **A.** Kurt Busch, who led 89 laps in the November 8, 2009, NASCAR premier series race at Texas Motor Speedway, beat Denny Hamlin to the finish line by 25.686 seconds, the largest margin of victory in the series at Texas.

326. **D.** Kyle Busch led 125 of the 267 laps in the inaugural NASCAR Sprint Cup Series race at Kentucky Speedway on July 9, 2011. He beat David Reutimann to the finish line by 0.179 seconds.

327. **C.** On January 21, 1973, Mark Donohue captured the checkered flag at Riverside International Raceway, more than one lap in front of Bobby Allison, to give Roger Penske his first victory in the NASCAR premier series.

328. **C.** AJ Allmendinger drove the final leg of the 2012 Rolex 24 At Daytona to help pilot the No. 60 Ford Riley to victory. Allmendinger split seat time with Oswaldo Negri, John Pew and Justin Wilson in the Michael Shank Racing with Curb-Agajanian race car.

329. **C.** In 1998, Greg Biffle finished eighth in the NASCAR Camping World Truck Series final points standings to win the Rookie of the Year. Three years later, in 2001, Biffle won five races and finished fourth in the final points standings in the NASCAR Nationwide Series to win the Rookie of the Year.

330. **B.** On February 23, 2003, Dave Blaney sat in the pole position of the NASCAR premier series race at Rockingham Speedway after posting a qualifying speed of 154.683 mph.

331. **A.** Dave Blaney, along with a couple of businessmen, purchased the Sharon Speedway in Hartford, Ohio, in 2002.

332. **B.** On September 16, 2007, Clint Bowyer led 222 of the 300 laps in the NASCAR Sprint Cup Series race at New Hampshire Motor Speedway, beating Jeff Gordon to the finish line by 6.469 seconds.

333. **C.** Jack Daniel's was the primary sponsor for Clint Bowyer's No. 07 Chevrolet in the NASCAR Sprint Cup Series from 2006 through 2008.

334. **C.** Denny Hamlin's pit crew on the Joe Gibbs–owned No. 11 FedEx Toyota won the 2011 NASCAR Sprint Pit Crew Challenge by beating the pit crew of Jimmie Johnson's No. 48 Lowe's Chevrolet, owned by Hendrick Motorsports. Hamlin's crew became the first to win back-to-back titles in the event.

335. **C.** On April 23, 2005, Kurt Busch stormed to victory at Phoenix International Raceway after leading 219 of 312 laps and beating Michael Waltrip to the finish line to earn the first perfect Driver Rating (150.0). NASCAR began keeping track of the stat in 2005 when they first began compiling Loop Data.

336. **A.** On March 24, 2002, Kurt Busch led 89 laps at Bristol Motor Speedway to capture the victory by 1.556 seconds over Jimmy Spencer. It was Kurt Busch's first of 24 victories in the NASCAR Sprint Cup Series (as of the beginning of the 2012 season).

337. **D.** On August 2, 2008, Circuit Gilles Villeneuve in Montreal hosted a NASCAR Nationwide Series race in the rain. Ron Fellows won the event. On August 12, 1959, Tim Flock won the first NASCAR premier series race held in the rain. The race was at Elkhart's Lake Road America in Wyoming.

338. **C.** New Hampshire Motor Speedway was built and financed by the Bob Bahre family, who owned it until 2008.

339. **B.** When Martinsville Speedway was resurfaced in 1979, it became the first track to use concrete.

340. **C.** Rusty Wallace provided assistance in deciding what the short track would look like when it opened in 2006.

341. **B.** In 1997, Roger Penske helped to build the two-mile super-speedway that was patterned after Michigan International Speedway.

342. **A.** On March 16, 1997, Las Vegas Motor Speedway hosted its first NASCAR Nationwide Series race, which was the first race

in the series to be held west of the Mississippi River. Jeff Green led 71 laps to win by a margin of 2.8 seconds over Dick Trickle.

343. **D.** On April 4, 1998, Dale Earnhardt Jr. earned his first victory in the NASCAR Nationwide Series at Texas Motor Speedway by 0.187 seconds over Elliott Sadler.

344. **B.** On September 18, 2011, Chicagoland Speedway hosted the first race in the Chase for the NASCAR Sprint Cup. Tony Stewart led 35 laps and beat Kevin Harvick to the finish line by 0.941 seconds for his first victory of the season.

345. **D.** On February 14, 1993, Dale Jarrett gave Joe Gibbs Racing its first victory in the NASCAR premier series at the Daytona 500. Jarrett captured the checkered flag by 0.16 seconds over Dale Earnhardt.

346. **C.** Thirty-five drivers are guaranteed spots in NASCAR Sprint Cup Series races based on owner's points, regardless of qualifying.

347. **A.** On September 6, 1965, Ned Jarrett, driving the No. 11 Ford, steered his race car to victory at Darlington Raceway more than 14 laps ahead of second-place finisher Buck Baker, a NASCAR premier series record that still stands today.

348. A. Benny Parsons first raced with an in-car camera during the 1979 Daytona 500. However, it wasn't until a couple years later that they became more common in NASCAR premier series race cars.

349. B. After winning races, Carl Edwards performs back flips off his race car's window sill in celebration of his victory.

350. C. Fonty Flock won the NASCAR Modified Tour in 1949, the series' second year. It was Flock's only championship in the series that was at that time called the NASCAR Modified Division.

351. D. Bobby Allison won the NASCAR Modified Tour championship in 1964 and 1965. Red Byron and Joe Weatherly won the championship in the series in 1948 and 1953, respectively. However, Bill Rexford never won the championship in the NASCAR Modified Tour.

352. A. German Quiroga won 3 consecutive NASCAR Toyota Series championships from 2009 through 2011. Quiroga has a total of 17 career wins in the series.

353. C. Andrew Ranger won the 2007 championship in the inaugural season of the NASCAR Canadian Tire Series behind the strength of one win and 10 top-10 finishes in 12 races.

354. C. In 1998, Kevin Harvick of Bakersfield, California, won the championship for what is now known as the NASCAR K&N Pro Series West. Harvick won five races and had 12 top-10 finishes in the series that season.

355. C. After the 2006 NASCAR season ended, Kyle Busch headed to Hawaii where he learned how to surf.

356. B. Danica Patrick appeared in 13 NASCAR Nationwide Series races in 2010, and 12 in 2011. She raced for Dale Earnhardt Jr.'s team, JR Motorsports. Her best finish was fourth place, achieved at Las Vegas Motor Speedway on March 5, 2011. In 2012, she will race full-time in the NASCAR Nationwide Series for JR Motorsports, and will compete in 10 races in the NASCAR Sprint Cup Series for Stewart-Haas Racing.

357. A. Dale Earnhardt Jr. started the Coca-Cola 600 on the pole on May 28, 2000, at Charlotte Motor Speedway. It was his first in the NASCAR premier series. He led 175 laps and finished fourth.

358. A. Carl Edwards won 3 races in 2003, his first full season in the NASCAR Camping World Truck Series. Two years later, he won 5 of 34 races during the NASCAR Nationwide Series season. Both years he was named the series Rookie of the Year.

359. B. Carl Edwards was a part-time substitute teacher and college student at the University of Missouri prior to signing with Roush Fenway Racing.

360. D. David Gilliland won the pole for the 2007 Daytona 500 by posting a qualifying speed of 186.320 mph. Gilliland led 18 laps and finished eighth in the Great American Race at Daytona International Speedway.

361. C. On May 29, 1994, Jeff Gordon started on the pole and led 16 laps of the Coca-Cola 600 at Charlotte Motor Speedway to earn his first victory in the NASCAR premier series. Gordon beat Rusty Wallace to the finish line by 3.91 seconds.

362. B. Jimmie Johnson is the only driver to qualify for every Chase for the NASCAR Sprint Cup. He finished in second place in 2004, fifth place in 2005, sixth place in 2011 and won the championship each year between 2006 and 2010.

363. C. On November 8, 2002, Kevin Harvick earned his first win in the NASCAR Camping World Truck Series as well as the first victory for Kevin Harvick Inc.

364. A. Kevin Harvick started the July 6, 2002, NASCAR premier series race at Daytona International Speedway on the pole. It was the first of his career in the series. He led 13 laps and finished 11th.

365. B. On September 27, 1998, Ricky Rudd won the NASCAR premier series race at Martinsville Speedway in his self-owned No. 10 Tide Ford. He beat Jeff Gordon to the finish line by 0.533 seconds. It was the last time a driver-owner won a race in the series until Tony Stewart won as a driver-owner on June 7, 2009, at Pocono Raceway.

366. D. Jimmie Johnson won both times the NASCAR premier series visited Dover International Speedway during his 2002 rookie season, capturing victories on June 2 and September 22.

367. C. On April 28, 2002, Jimmie Johnson earned his first victory in the NASCAR premier series at Auto Club Speedway. He led 62 laps and beat Kurt Busch to the finish line by 0.620 seconds.

368. C. Kasey Kahne appeared in all 36 races of the 2011 NASCAR Sprint Cup Series season racing in the No. 4 Red Bull Toyota for Red Bull Racing. He won one race and two poles.

369. B. Sam Bass, who is the first Officially Licensed Artist for NASCAR, designed the 2007 NASCAR Day lapel pin that could be purchased for $5.

370. A. While Keith Urban has performed at the Daytona 500, he has never been a NASCAR Day spokesperson.

371. D. On May 14, 2005, Kasey Kahne earned his first victory in the NASCAR premier series. The race was run at Richmond International Raceway. Kahne led for 242 laps and beat Tony Stewart to the finish line by 1.674 seconds.

372. B. On May 28, 2000, Matt Kenseth earned his first victory in the NASCAR premier series at Charlotte Motor Speedway leading 32 laps and beating Bobby Labonte to the finish line by 0.573 seconds.

373. B. Brad Keselowski made two starts in the 2008 NASCAR Sprint Cup Series season and then in his third start of the 2009 season on April 26, 2009, he beat Dale Earnhardt Jr. to the finish line by 0.175 seconds for his first win in the series.

374. A. Jimmie Johnson has won at least one race in every Chase for the NASCAR Sprint Cup between 2004 and 2011. In 2004, 2007 and 2009, Johnson won four races in each Chase.

375. B. On September 19, 2004, Kurt Busch led 155 of 300 laps to win the first Chase for the NASCAR Sprint Cup race, which was held at New Hampshire Motor Speedway. Busch went on to capture the NASCAR premier series championship that year.

376. C. Brad Keselowski started on the pole for the September 19, 2010, NASCAR Sprint Cup Series race at New Hampshire

Motor Speedway. It was his first pole in the series and he set a track qualifying record, which was broken by Ryan Newman the following year.

377. C. Travis Kvapil appeared in a June 2006 episode of *The Guiding Light* as himself. The episode was taped at Hickory Motor Speedway in North Carolina.

378. B. On November 16, 2003, Bobby Labonte won his most recent race in the NASCAR premier series as of the beginning of the 2012 season. The race was run at Homestead-Miami Speedway. Labonte beat Kevin Harvick to the finish line by 1.749 seconds.

379. C. Joey Logano sat on the pole for the March 21, 2010, NASCAR Sprint Cup Series race at Bristol Motor Speedway. He was 19 years, 9 months and 25 days, making him the youngest pole winner in the series.

380. A. Harry Gant sat on the pole for the August 27, 1994, NASCAR premier series race at Bristol Motor Speedway, which made him the oldest driver in the series to win a pole at 54 years, 7 months and 17 days.

381. C. Mark Martin started the July 11, 1981, NASCAR premier series race at Nashville Speedway on the pole. He led 36 laps and finished 11th.

382. **A.** On October 26, 2002, Jamie McMurray became the 100th different driver to win in the NASCAR Nationwide Series after his victory at Atlanta Motor Speedway.

383. **B.** In only his second start in the NASCAR premier series, Jamie McMurray won the October 13, 2002, race at Charlotte Motor Speedway. McMurray led 96 laps and beat Bobby Labonte to the finish line by 0.35 seconds.

384. **C.** On April 3, 1999, Ron Hornaday Jr. led 185 of the 200 laps in the NASCAR Camping World Truck Series race at Evergreen Speedway in Monroe, Washington. The race was the 100th in the series. Hornaday beat Jack Sprague to the finish line by 2.509 seconds.

385. **D.** In 2006, Casey Mears earned the overall win in the Rolex 24 At Daytona. Mears teamed with Scott Dixon and Dan Wheldon in a car owned by Target Ganassi Racing.

386. **C.** Paul Menard started the July 5, 2008, race at Daytona International Speedway on the pole. Menard led 19 laps and finished 15th.

387. **A.** Joe Nemechek studied mechanical engineering at the Florida Institute of Technology in Melbourne, Florida, before focusing on racing full-time.

388. D. On September 19, 1999, Joe Nemechek led 72 of 300 laps at New Hampshire Motor Speedway to earn his first win in the NASCAR premier series.

389. A. Tony Stewart, as well as Dale Earnhardt Jr., appeared in the music video "The Road I'm On" by 3 Doors Down.

390. B. Tony Stewart, along with Kyle Petty, was named by *USA Weekend Magazine* as one of 2004's Most Caring Athletes.

391. B. On September 11, 1999, Tony Stewart earned his first victory in the NASCAR premier series. The race was run at Richmond International Raceway, where Stewart led 333 of the 400 laps and beat Bobby Labonte to the finish line by 1.115 seconds.

392. C. At the age of 20 in 2003, Brian Vickers became the youngest champion among the three NASCAR national touring series when he won the NASCAR Nationwide Series title behind the strength of three victories.

393. A. Brian Vickers started ninth in the October 8, 2006, race at Talladega Superspeedway. However, he led 17 of the 188 laps and held the lead in front of Kasey Kahne when the race ended under caution.

394. D. J.J. Yeley started on the pole for the June 17, 2007, race at

Michigan International Speedway. Yeley finished 28th in the race.

395. D. On September 16, 2001, Robby Gordon led 17 of the 300 laps at New Hampshire Motor Speedway to win by 2.008 seconds over second-place finisher Sterling Marlin.

396. A. Dale Jarrett was offered a full scholarship to play golf at the University of South Carolina in Columbia, South Carolina.

397. B. Bob Osborne, Carl Edwards' crew chief, won the 2011 DIRECTV Crew Chief of the Year, which is awarded to the crew chief of the driver who has demonstrated the best qualifying and race effort based on finishing positions.

398. A. Carl Edwards' pit crew on the No. 99 Roush Fenway Racing Ford won the 2011 Mechanix Wear Most Valuable Pit Crew Award, which is determined by a vote from each team's crew chief.

399. D. Tony Stewart won the most Mobil 1 Driver of the Race Awards in 2011. The weekly prize is given to the winner of each NASCAR Sprint Cup Series race. Since Stewart won more races in 2011 than any other driver, he was also presented the season-ending Mobil 1 Driver of the Race Award.

400. C. The race, which took place on July 10, 1938, was Bill France's first venture into promoting stock car races. It provided France and his partner, Charlie Reese, a $200 profit to be split between the two.

401. **A.** On November 20, 1977, Janet Guthrie led five laps in the NASCAR premier series race at Ontario Motor Speedway in California. Guthrie finished the race 25 laps down in 24th place driving the No. 68 Kelly Girl Chevrolet.

402. **D.** Curtis Turner and Bruton Smith partnered to build the Charlotte Motor Speedway in 1959.

403. **B.** Dale Earnhardt has nine career wins in the NASCAR premier series at Atlanta Motor Speedway. Cale Yarborough is second with seven wins.

404. **D.** Buddy Baker and Ryan Newman both have seven career poles in the NASCAR premier series at Atlanta Motor Speedway. Cale Yarborough is next with six poles at the 1.54-mile track.

405. **A.** On November 15, 1997, Geoff Bodine set the NASCAR premier series qualifying record at Atlanta Motor Speedway with a speed of 197.478 mph. Bodine led four laps and finished 33rd.

406. **A.** On November 16, 1997, Bobby Labonte set the NASCAR

premier series race record at Atlanta Motor Speedway with a speed of 159.904 mph. Labonte led 168 of the 325 laps and beat Dale Jarrett to the finish line by 3.801 seconds.

407. C. Wood Brothers' drivers have tallied a total of 12 wins in the NASCAR premier series at Atlanta Motor Speedway. Hendrick Motorsports is second with 11 wins.

408. A. Jimmie Johnson holds the record for the most NASCAR premier series wins at Auto Club Speedway with five. Jeff Gordon and Matt Kenseth are tied for second with three apiece.

409. D. Kurt Busch holds the record for the most NASCAR premier series poles at Auto Club Speedway with three. Jeff Gordon, Denny Hamlin, Jamie McMurray and Brian Vickers are all tied with two poles apiece.

410. A. On February 25, 2005, Kyle Busch set the NASCAR premier series qualifying record at Auto Club Speedway with a speed of 188.245 mph. Busch finished 23rd after leading only two laps.

411. C. On June 22, 1997, Jeff Gordon set the NASCAR premier series race record at Auto Club Speedway with a speed of 155.012 mph. Gordon led 113 laps and beat Terry Labonte to the finish line by 1.074 seconds.

MULTIPLE CHOICE ANSWER KEY

412. **A.** Darrell Waltrip has 12 career NASCAR premier series victories at Bristol Motor Speedway, which is 3 more than the drivers with the second most at Bristol: Dale Earnhardt, Rusty Wallace and Cale Yarborough.

413. **D.** Junior Johnson Racing's drivers have accumulated 16 wins in the NASCAR premier series at Bristol Motor Speedway. Roush Fenway Racing is second with 10.

414. **C.** Cale Yarborough and Mark Martin both have nine poles in the NASCAR premier series at Bristol Motor Speedway. Rusty Wallace has the next most with seven.

415. **B.** On March 21, 2003, Ryan Newman set the NASCAR premier series qualifying record at Bristol Motor Speedway with a speed of 128.709 mph. Newman finished the race in 22nd place.

416. **C.** On July 11, 1971, Charlie Glotzbach set the NASCAR premier series race record at Bristol Motor Speedway with a speed of 101.074 mph. Glotzbach led 411 laps and beat Bobby Allison to the finish line by more than 3 laps.

417. **A.** Jimmie Johnson is tied with Bobby Allison and Darrell Waltrip with six points wins in the NASCAR premier series at Charlotte Motor Speedway.

418. C. Hendrick Motorsports' drivers have twice as many wins (16) in the NASCAR premier series than the next two teams. Richard Petty's drivers have a combined 8 wins at the track, as do Roush Fenway Racing's drivers.

419. B. David Pearson has a total of 14 poles in the NASCAR premier series at Charlotte Motor Speedway. Ryan Newman and Jeff Gordon are second and third with 9 and 8 poles, respectively.

420. B. On October 13, 2005, Elliott Sadler set the NASCAR premier series qualifying record at Charlotte Motor Speedway with a speed of 193.216 mph. Sadler led 112 laps and finished 27th.

421. A. On October 11, 1999, Jeff Gordon set the NASCAR premier series race record for a 500-mile event at Charlotte Motor Speedway with a speed of 160.306 mph. Gordon led 16 laps and beat Bobby Labonte to the finish line by 0.851 seconds.

422. A. Tony Stewart has won three times in the NASCAR premier series at Chicagoland Speedway, with the most recent victory coming in 2011. Kevin Harvick is second with two wins.

423. A. Joe Gibbs Racing's drivers have won three times in the NASCAR premier series at Chicagoland Speedway, while

Richard Childress Racing and Hendrick Motorsports' drivers have won twice at the track.

424. **D.** On July 8, 2005, Jimmie Johnson set the NASCAR premier series qualifying record at Chicagoland Speedway with a speed of 188.147 mph. Johnson led 21 laps and finished third.

425. **B.** On July 10, 2010, David Reutimann set the NASCAR Sprint Cup Series race record at Chicagoland Speedway with a speed of 145.138 mph. Reutimann led 52 laps and beat Carl Edwards to the finish line by 0.727 seconds.

426. **D.** David Pearson has twice as many poles (12) in the NASCAR premier series at Darlington Raceway than the next two drivers, Fred Lorenzen and Glenn "Fireball" Roberts, who both have 6 poles at the track.

427. **A.** Hendrick Motorsports' drivers have won 13 times in the NASCAR premier series at Darlington Raceway. Junior Johnson Racing is second with 9 victories at the track.

428. **B.** On May 6, 2011, Kasey Kahne set the NASCAR Sprint Cup Series qualifying record at Darlington Raceway with a speed of 181.254 mph. Kahne led 124 laps and finished fourth.

429. **C.** On May 10, 2008, Kyle Busch set the NASCAR Sprint Cup

Series race record at Darlington Raceway with a speed of 140.350 mph. Busch beat Carl Edwards to the finish line by 3.115 seconds.

430. B. Cale Yarborough has double the number of poles (12) in the NASCAR premier series at Daytona International Speedway than the driver with the next most, Glenn "Fireball" Roberts (6).

431. A. Richard Petty has 10 victories in points-paying events in the NASCAR premier series at Daytona International Speedway. Cale Yarborough is second with 9.

432. C. Wood Brothers' drivers have earned 15 trips to Victory Lane in the NASCAR premier series at Daytona International Speedway. Richard Petty's drivers are second with 11 checkered flags.

433. A. On July 4, 1980, Bobby Allison set the NASCAR premier series race record for a 400-mile event at Daytona International Speedway with a speed of 173.473 mph. Allison beat David Pearson to the finish line by one second.

434. D. On February 17, 1980, Buddy Baker set the NASCAR premier series race record for a 500-mile event at Daytona International Speedway with a speed of 177.602 mph. Baker led 143 of the 200 laps and was in the lead when the race ended under caution.

MULTIPLE CHOICE ANSWER KEY

435. B. David Pearson has claimed six poles in the NASCAR premier series at Dover International Speedway. Rusty Wallace is second with five poles at the track.

436. B. Bobby Allison and Richard Petty both have seven wins in the NASCAR premier series at Dover International Speedway. Jimmie Johnson is second with six victories at the one-mile track.

437. D. Hendrick Motorsports' drivers have won 13 races in the NASCAR premier series at Dover International Speedway. Roush Fenway Racing is in second with nine victories.

438. C. On June 4, 2004, Jeremy Mayfield set the NASCAR premier series qualifying record at Dover International Speedway with a speed of 161.522 mph. Mayfield led 78 laps and finished eighth in the race.

439. B. On September 21, 1997, Mark Martin set the NASCAR premier series race record at Dover International Speedway with a speed of 132.719 mph. Martin won by 10.334 seconds over Dale Earnhardt.

440. C. Jamie McMurray has only one pole in the NASCAR premier series at Homestead-Miami Speedway, while Kurt Busch, Carl Edwards, Jimmie Johnson and Kasey Kahne all have earned two.

441. **A.** Greg Biffle and Tony Stewart both have three NASCAR premier series wins at Homestead-Miami Speedway. Carl Edwards is second with two victories at the track.

442. **B.** On November 14, 2003, Jamie McMurray set the NASCAR premier series qualifying record at Homestead-Miami Speedway with a speed of 181.111 mph. McMurray did not lead any laps during the race and finished ninth.

443. **D.** On November 14, 1999, Tony Stewart set the NASCAR premier series race record at Homestead-Miami Speedway with a speed of 140.335 mph. Stewart beat Bobby Labonte to the finish line by 5.289 seconds.

444. **A.** Jeff Gordon has a total of three poles in the NASCAR premier series at Indianapolis Motor Speedway. Ernie Irvan has the second most with two.

445. **B.** Jeff Gordon has a record four wins in the NASCAR premier series at Indianapolis Motor Speedway. Jimmie Johnson is second with three victories at the track.

446. **D.** On August 7, 2004, Casey Mears set the NASCAR premier series qualifying record at Indianapolis Motor Speedway with a speed of 186.293 mph. Mears led two laps and finished the race in 26th.

447. **D.** On August 5, 2000, Bobby Labonte set the NASCAR premier series race record at Indianapolis Motor Speedway with a speed of 155.912 mph. Labonte led 21 of the 160 laps and beat Rusty Wallace by 4.229 seconds.

448. **A.** Jeff Gordon has five NASCAR premier series poles at Sonoma, while Ricky Rudd is second with four.

449. **D.** Jeff Gordon has claimed a record of five career victories in the NASCAR premier series at Sonoma. Ernie Irvan, Ricky Rudd, Tony Stewart and Rusty Wallace are tied with two wins apiece.

450. **D.** On June 24, 2005, Jeff Gordon set the NASCAR premier series qualifying speed record at Sonoma with a speed of 94.325 mph. Gordon led 32 laps and finished 33rd in the race.

451. **B.** On June 23, 2002, Ricky Rudd set the NASCAR premier series race record at Sonoma with a speed of 81.007 mph. Rudd beat Tony Stewart to the checkered flag by 2.487 seconds after only leading three laps.

452. **B.** Jimmie Johnson has a record three NASCAR premier series poles at Kansas Speedway. Kasey Kahne is second with two poles at the track.

453. **A.** Greg Biffle, Jeff Gordon, Jimmie Johnson and Tony Stewart have all won twice in the NASCAR premier series at Kansas Speedway, while Ryan Newman has only won once.

454. **D.** On October 8, 2005, Matt Kenseth set the NASCAR premier series qualifying record at Kansas Speedway with a speed of 180.856 mph. Kenseth led 71 laps and placed fifth in the race.

455. **C.** On October 3, 2010, Greg Biffle set the NASCAR Sprint Cup Series race record at Kansas Speedway with a speed of 138.077 mph. Biffle led 60 of the 267 laps to beat Jimmie Johnson to the finish line by 7.638 seconds.

456. **D.** Qualifying for the inaugural NASCAR Sprint Cup Series race at Kentucky Speedway was cancelled because of rain.

457. **B.** Roush Fenway Racing has seven wins at Las Vegas Motor Speedway in the NASCAR premier series among its drivers. Hendrick Motorsports is second with five wins.

458. **C.** Jimmie Johnson has won four NASCAR premier series races at Las Vegas Motor Speedway, the most recent one coming in 2010. Jeff Burton, Carl Edwards and Matt Kenseth are tied for second with two wins apiece.

MULTIPLE CHOICE ANSWER KEY

459. A. On March 9, 2012, Kasey Kahne set the NASCAR Sprint Cup Series qualifying record at Las Vegas Motor Speedway with a speed of 190.456 mph. Kahne didn't lead any laps during the race and finished 19th.

460. D. On March 1, 1998, Mark Martin set the NASCAR premier series race record at Las Vegas Motor Speedway with a speed of 146.554 mph. Martin beat Jeff Burton to the finish line by 1.605 seconds.

461. C. Richard Petty won a record 15 NASCAR premier series races at Martinsville Speedway. Darrell Waltrip is in second place with 11 victories.

462. B. Darrell Waltrip leads the way with eight career poles in the NASCAR premier series at Martinsville Speedway. Geoff Bodine and Jeff Gordon share second place with seven poles apiece.

463. B. Petty Enterprises' drivers have claimed 19 wins in the NASCAR premier series at Martinsville Speedway, while Hendrick Motorsports has 18 victories at the track.

464. A. On October 21, 2005, Tony Stewart set the NASCAR premier series qualifying speed record at Martinsville Speedway with a speed of 98.083 mph. Stewart finished second to Jeff Gordon in the race after leading 283 laps.

465. **A.** On September 22, 1996, Jeff Gordon set the NASCAR premier series race record at Martinsville Speedway with a speed of 82.223 mph. Gordon won the race 0.49 seconds ahead of Terry Labonte.

466. **D.** David Pearson has a record 10 poles in the NASCAR premier series at Michigan International Speedway. Bill Elliott is second with 6 poles at the track.

467. **C.** David Pearson has a record nine victories in the NASCAR premier series at Michigan International Speedway, with his last victory at the track occurring in 1978. Cale Yarborough is second with eight wins at the track.

468. **A.** On June 18, 2005, Ryan Newman set the NASCAR premier series qualifying speed record at Michigan International Speedway with a speed of 194.232 mph. Newman finished the race in 15th place after leading three laps.

469. **A.** On June 13, 1999, Dale Jarrett set the NASCAR premier series race record at Michigan International Speedway with a speed of 173.997 mph. Jarrett led 150 of the 200 laps and beat Jeff Gordon to the checkers by 0.505 seconds.

470. **D.** Jeff Burton has a record four victories in the NASCAR premier series at New Hampshire Motor Speedway. Kurt

Busch, Jeff Gordon, Jimmie Johnson, Ryan Newman and Tony Stewart are all tied with three.

471. C. Ryan Newman has twice as many poles (six) in the NASCAR premier series at New Hampshire Motor Speedway than the next driver, Jeff Gordon (three).

472. A. On July 13, 1997, Jeff Burton set the NASCAR premier series race record at New Hampshire Motor Speedway with a speed of 117.134 mph. He beat Dale Earnhardt to the checkers by 5.372 seconds.

473. C. On July 15, 2011, Ryan Newman set the NASCAR premier series qualifying speed record at New Hampshire Motor Speedway with a speed of 135.232 mph. Newman led 119 of the 301 laps and went on to claim the victory over Tony Stewart.

474. B. Ryan Newman has a record four NASCAR premier series poles at Phoenix International Raceway. Carl Edwards, Jeff Gordon and Rusty Wallace are all tied for second with three poles apiece.

475. B. Jimmie Johnson has won a record four races in the NASCAR premier series at Phoenix International Raceway. His most recent victory at the track came in 2009.

476. **A.** On February 26, 2011, Carl Edwards set the NASCAR premier series qualifying speed record at Phoenix International Raceway with a speed of 137.279 mph. Edwards finished 28th in the race after leading 21 laps.

477. **D.** On November 7, 1999, Tony Stewart set the NASCAR premier series race record at Phoenix International Raceway with a speed of 118.132 mph. He led 154 laps and beat Mark Martin to the finish line by 2.081 seconds.

478. **C.** Bill Elliott and Ken Schrader both have a record five poles in the NASCAR premier series at Pocono Raceway. Mark Martin, Rusty Wallace, Darrell Waltrip and Cale Yarborough are all tied for second with three poles apiece.

479. **A.** Jeff Gordon and Bill Elliott both have a record five victories in the NASCAR premier series at Pocono Raceway. Denny Hamlin, Tim Richmond, Rusty Wallace and Darrell Waltrip are all tied for second with four wins apiece.

480. **B.** On June 11, 2004, Kasey Kahne posted a new NASCAR premier series qualifying speed record at Pocono Raceway with a speed of 172.533 mph. Kahne led four laps and finished 14th in the race.

481. **C.** On June 12, 2011, Jeff Gordon set the NASCAR Sprint Cup Series race record at Pocono Raceway with a speed of 145.384 mph.

He led 39 laps and beat second-place finisher Kurt Busch to the checkers by 2.965 seconds.

482. **B.** Richard Petty has almost twice as many wins (13) at Richmond International Raceway than the next driver, Bobby Allison (7). David Pearson, Rusty Wallace and Darrell Waltrip are tied for third with 6 wins apiece.

483. **B.** Bobby Allison and Richard Petty are tied with eight poles apiece in the NASCAR premier series at Richmond International Raceway. Darrell Waltrip is next with seven poles at the short track.

484. **D.** Petty Enterprises' drivers have won 15 times in the NASCAR premier series at Richmond International Raceway. Hendrick Motorsports is second with 10 victories.

485. **A.** On May 14, 2004, Brian Vickers set the NASCAR premier series qualifying record at Richmond International Raceway with a speed of 129.983 mph. Vickers led 32 laps and finished eighth in the race.

486. **A.** On September 6, 1997, Dale Jarrett set the NASCAR premier series race record at Richmond International Raceway with a speed of 109.047 mph. He led 39 laps and beat Jeff Burton to the finish line by 1.802 seconds.

487. C. Bill Elliott's last pole at Talladega Superspeedway came in 1993, but he leads all NASCAR premier series drivers with eight total poles at the track. Cale Yarborough is second with six.

488. D. Dale Earnhardt has a total of 10 victories in the NASCAR premier series at Talladega Superspeedway. His final victory at the track on October 15, 2000, was his last in the series.

489. D. Richard Childress Racing's drivers have scored 12 victories at Talladega Superspeedway in the NASCAR premier series, one more win than Hendrick Motorsports.

490. B. On May 10, 1997, Mark Martin set the NASCAR premier series race record at Talladega Superspeedway with a speed of 188.354 mph. Martin led 47 laps and beat Dale Earnhardt to the checkers by 0.146 seconds. The race was originally scheduled for April 27, but was postponed because of rain.

491. B. Dale Earnhardt Jr., Bobby Labonte and Ryan Newman each have two poles at Texas Motor Speedway, but Kenny Irwin Jr. has one pole, which came in 1999.

492. A. Roush Fenway Racing has eight victories at Texas Motor Speedway as of the start of the 2012 season.

493. D. On November 3, 2006, Brian Vickers set the NASCAR premier series qualifying record at Texas Motor Speedway with a speed of 196.235 mph. Vickers led five laps and finished 27th in the race.

494. B. On November 6, 2011, Tony Stewart set the NASCAR Sprint Cup Series race record at Texas Motor Speedway with a speed of 152.705 mph. He beat Carl Edwards to the finish line by 1.092 seconds.

495. C. Tony Stewart has five wins in the NASCAR premier series at Watkins Glen International, his last victory at the track coming in 2009. Jeff Gordon is in second place with four victories at the road course.

496. B. Mark Martin and Dale Earnhardt have both earned three poles in the NASCAR premier series at Watkins Glen International. Jeff Gordon and Terry Labonte are tied for second with two poles apiece.

497. A. On August 13, 2011, Kyle Busch set the NASCAR Sprint Cup Series qualifying record at Watkins Glen International with a speed of 126.421 mph. Busch led 49 laps and finished third in the race.

498. A. On August 13, 1995, Mark Martin posted a NASCAR

premier series race speed record at Watkins Glen International with a speed of 103.030 mph. Martin led 61 of the 90 laps to beat Wally Dallenbach Jr. by 1.01 seconds.

499. B. After winning the 1989 Daytona 500, Darrell Waltrip broke out his rendition of the Ickey Shuffle, which was the touchdown celebration of Ickey Woods of the Cincinatti Bengals in the NFL.

500. A. Sunoco provides each race team with free gas during the race weekend.

501. A. On February 17, 2008, Ryan Newman started 7th in the 50th running of the Great American Race and led eight laps to beat Kurt Busch to the finish line by 0.092 seconds.

502. C. NASCAR and NASCAR Hall of Fame licensee, Jostens, design and create the rings that NASCAR Hall of Fame inductees receive at their Induction Ceremony.

503. C. As of the beginning of the 2012 season, Jeff Gordon has won 12 restrictor-plate races in the NASCAR Sprint Cup Series. Dale Earnhardt has 11 victories in these races, while Jimmie Johnson and Richard Petty have 3 and zero, respectively.

504. A. Johnny Rutherford of Fort Worth, Texas, drove the No. 13 race car to its only victory in the NASCAR premier series. The race was run at Daytona International Speedway on February 22, 1963.

505. **B.** Joe Nemechek of Lakeland, Florida, drove the No. 01 race car to its only victory in the NASCAR premier series. The race was run at Kansas Speedway on October 10, 2004.

506. **B.** On February 26, 1967, Mario Andretti led 112 of 200 laps to win the Daytona 500 and become the 100th different driver to win in the NASCAR premier series.

507. **D.** Brad Keselowski of Rochester Hills, Michigan, drove the No. 09 race car to its only victory in the NASCAR premier series. The race was run at Talladega Superspeedway on April 26, 2009.

508. **A.** Speedy Thompson of Monroe, North Carolina, drove the No. 30 race car to its only victory in the NASCAR premier series. The race was run at Martinsville Speedway on October 16, 1955.

509. **D.** Bobby Isaac of Catawba, North Carolina, drove the No. 37 race car to its only victory in the NASCAR premier series. The race was run at Columbia Speedway (South Carolina) on April 18, 1968.

510. **A.** Bob Burdick of Omaha, Nebraska, drove the No. 53 race car to its only victory in the NASCAR premier series. The race was run at Atlanta Motor Speedway on March 26, 1961.

MULTIPLE CHOICE ANSWER KEY

511. C. On March 27, 1966, Jim Hurtubise drove the No. 56 race car to its only victory in the NASCAR premier series. The race was run at Atlanta Motor Speedway. Hurtubise finished ahead of second-place finisher Fred Lorenzen by more than one lap.

512. B. Johnny Allen of Greenville, South Carolina, drove the No. 58 race car to its only victory in the NASCAR premier series on June 16, 1962. Allen beat Rex White by only six inches in the race at Bowman Gray Stadium in Winston-Salem, North Carolina.

513. B. On May 30, 1950, Bill Rexford steered the No. 60 race car to its only victory in the NASCAR premier series. The race was run at Canfield Fairgrounds in Ohio.

514. A. On September 3, 1962, Larry Frank piloted the No. 66 race car to its only victory in the NASCAR premier series by beating Junior Johnson to the finish line by five seconds at Darlington Raceway.

515. D. Frankie Schneider earned the No. 62 race car its only victory in the NASCAR premier series. The race was run on April 25, 1958, at Old Dominion Speedway in Manassas, Virginia. The second-place finisher was Jack Smith.

516. B. Joe Lee Johnson earned the No. 77 race car its only victory in the NASCAR premier series. The race was run on August 9, 1959, at Nashville Speedway in Lebanon, Tennessee. Johnson beat Larry Frank to the finish line by more than three laps.

517. A. On October 18, 1953, Jim Paschal piloted the No. 80 race car to its only victory in the NASCAR premier series. The race was held at Martinsville Speedway in Virginia.

518. D. Danny Graves earned the No. 81 race car its only victory in the NASCAR premier series. The race was held on September 8, 1957, at California State Fairgrounds in Sacramento.

519. C. Buck Baker took the checkers at the June 23, 1961, NASCAR premier series race at Hartsville Speedway in South Carolina. Baker was behind the steering wheel of the No. 86 Chrysler, which is the only victory in the series for the No. 86 race car.

520. A. On May 17, 1981, Jody Ridley piloted the No. 90 Truxmore/ Sunny King Ford to a first-place finish in the NASCAR premier series race, leading 180 of the 500 laps. He finished 22 seconds ahead of runner-up Bobby Allison. It's the only victory in the series for the No. 90 race car.

TRUE/FALSE

1. The longest track currently hosting a NASCAR Sprint Cup Series event is Talladega Superspeedway at 2.66 miles long.

TRUE   FALSE

2. NASCAR was incorporated on December 14, 1947.

TRUE   FALSE

3. The headquarters for NASCAR is located in Charlotte, North Carolina.

TRUE   FALSE

4. The track that hosted the last NASCAR premier series race featuring convertibles was Darlington Raceway.

TRUE   FALSE

5. The record for the most lead changes in a NASCAR Sprint Cup Series race is 87.

TRUE   FALSE

6. Tony Stewart is the first driver-owner to win the NASCAR Sprint Cup Series championship.

      TRUE   FALSE

7. Trevor Bayne's victory in the 2011 Daytona 500 gave Ford its 600th win.

      TRUE   FALSE

8. What is typically referred to as the "modern era" of NASCAR began in 1972.

      TRUE   FALSE

9. The No. 43 race car has more wins combined between the NASCAR Sprint Cup, NASCAR Nationwide and NASCAR Camping World Truck Series than any other race car number.

      TRUE   FALSE

10. David Pearson has the highest winning percentage of drivers in the NASCAR Sprint Cup Series.

    TRUE   **FALSE**

11. Soldier Field, which is home to the NFL's Chicago Bears, hosted a NASCAR premier series race in 1956.

    TRUE   **FALSE**

12. Jeff Gordon reached his 50th win in the NASCAR Sprint Cup Series in fewer races than any other driver.

    TRUE   **FALSE**

13. When Tony Stewart won the Ford 400 at Homestead-Miami Speedway in 2011 it was the sixth time a series champion won the season finale in his championship season.

    TRUE   **FALSE**

14. NASCAR ran its first race on the Daytona Beach & Road Course before NASCAR was even incorporated.

　　　TRUE　　**FALSE**

15. NASCAR Sprint Cup Series driver Joey Logano was able to successfully complete the Atomic Bomb Challenge on an episode of *Man v. Food Nation*.

　　　TRUE　　**FALSE**

16. Junior Johnson is credited with discovering how to draft on his way to winning the 1960 Daytona 500.

　　　TRUE　　**FALSE**

17. NASCAR sanctions two international series outside of the United States.

　　　TRUE　　**FALSE**

18. Every year between 1949 and 1978, Petty Enterprises had at least one car win a race in the NASCAR premier series.

    TRUE   **FALSE**

19. In 1969, LeeRoy Yarbrough was the first driver to win what was called NASCAR's "Triple Crown" – the Daytona 500, the Coca-Cola 600 and the Southern 500.

    TRUE   **FALSE**

20. In 1959, the first Daytona 500 was run caution-free.

    TRUE   **FALSE**

21. Race cars have always been allowed to pit under caution and refuel in NASCAR-sanctioned races.

    TRUE   **FALSE**

22. Maurice Petty never raced in the NASCAR premier series, preferring to work behind the scenes on the engines of his father and brother's race cars.

TRUE   FALSE

23. Kyle Busch's victory in the Sony HD 500 at Auto Club Speedway on September 4, 2005, makes him the youngest race winner in the NASCAR premier series.

TRUE   FALSE

24. The meeting in Daytona Beach, Florida, between the nation's best drivers, car owners, race promoters and mechanics to discuss the future of stock car racing lasted four days.

TRUE   FALSE

25. There were three Flock siblings who competed in NASCAR-sanctioned events.

TRUE   FALSE

26. Indy cars have never competed at Darlington Raceway in South Carolina.

    TRUE   **FALSE**

27. Some NASCAR drivers are superstitious about driving race cars with green paint schemes.

    TRUE   **FALSE**

28. Terry Cook has the most consecutive race starts in the NASCAR Camping World Truck Series with 296.

    TRUE   **FALSE**

29. For the first time in NASCAR history, every race during the 1990 NASCAR premier series season was televised live.

    TRUE   **FALSE**

30. In October 1993, Harry Gant earned the nickname "Mr. October" after winning four consecutive races in the month.

   TRUE   **FALSE**

31. No driver has ever been awarded a NASCAR series championship in any NASCAR series posthumously.

   TRUE   **FALSE**

32. AJ Allmendinger's first pole award in the NASCAR Sprint Cup Series was for the April 10, 2010, race at Phoenix International Raceway.

   TRUE   **FALSE**

33. Richie Evans is the only driver to win nine NASCAR championships.

   TRUE   **FALSE**

34. Johnny Benson and Greg Biffle are the only two drivers, going into the 2012 season, to have won championships in both the NASCAR Nationwide and NASCAR Camping World Truck Series.

   TRUE   FALSE

35. Martin Truex Jr. won the inaugural race at Autodromo Hermanos Rodriguez in what is now the NASCAR Nationwide Series.

   TRUE   FALSE

36. Richard Petty played wide receiver on Randleman High School's football team growing up.

   TRUE   FALSE

37. NASCAR races often draw larger crowds than a Super Bowl, NBA Finals game or World Series game.

   TRUE   FALSE

38. NASCAR annually sanctions a couple hundred races at around 75 tracks across more than 30 U.S. states, Canada and Mexico.

TRUE   FALSE

39. Cale Yarborough is the only NASCAR premier series driver to steer the No. 06 car to Victory Lane in the series.

TRUE   FALSE

40. The NASCAR industry participates in the second largest recycling program in all of sports.

TRUE   FALSE

41. Former NASCAR premier series champion Alan Kulwicki only had six career victories in the series.

TRUE   FALSE

42. As of the end of the 2011 season, brothers Terry and Bobby Labonte were tied with 22 career wins apiece in the NASCAR Sprint Cup Series.

TRUE   **FALSE**

43. Indianapolis Motor Speedway has part of an 18-hole, par-72, golf course in its infield.

TRUE   **FALSE**

44. The History Channel show *American Pickers* featured an episode where the two hosts picked items for possible display in the NASCAR Hall of Fame.

TRUE   **FALSE**

45. As of the end of the 2011 season, Tony Stewart holds the record for the most NASCAR Sprint Cup Series victories on road courses with seven trips to Victory Lane.

TRUE   **FALSE**

46. Richard and Kyle Petty are co-chairmen and co-CEOs for Victory Junction, which is a camp for children with chronic medical conditions or serious illnesses, located in Randleman, North Carolina.

TRUE   FALSE

47. Dale Earnhardt Jr. has buffalo on his property in Mooresville, North Carolina.

TRUE   FALSE

48. Adam Sandler and Kevin James gave the command "Gentlemen, start your engines!" at Michigan International Speedway in 2010. They were promoting their movie, *I Now Pronounce You Chuck & Larry*.

TRUE   FALSE

49. Darrell Waltrip played a vehicular version of himself in the hit movie *Cars* providing the voice for the character Darrell Cartrip.

TRUE   FALSE

50. Homestead-Miami Speedway was turned into a Hollywood set to film an episode of A&E's *The Glades.*

    TRUE   **FALSE**

51. Jeff Gordon has appeared as a co-host or guest on *Live with Regis and Kelly* 10 times.

    TRUE   **FALSE**

52. 2011 NASCAR Camping World Truck Series champion Austin Dillon competed that season in a truck owned by his grandfather, Richard Childress.

    TRUE   **FALSE**

53. NASCAR Sprint Cup Series events at Sonoma have 11 turns.

    TRUE   **FALSE**

54. NASCAR Publishing had a long-standing partnership with Harlequin to publish a series of NASCAR-licensed romance novels.

 TRUE   FALSE

55. *NASCAR Unleashed*, the NASCAR-licensed video game created by Activision and released in November 2011, allows competitors to leave the traditional NASCAR-sanctioned venues behind and race on streets, sidewalks, beaches and off-road areas outside the tracks.

 TRUE   FALSE

56. Talladega Superspeedway and Daytona International Speedway are the only two tracks on the NASCAR Sprint Cup Series schedule that have restrictor-plate racing.

 TRUE   FALSE

57. Santa Fe Speedway, which hosted one race in the NASCAR premier series on July 10, 1954, is the largest track in the state of New Mexico.

 TRUE   FALSE

58. Fonty Flock won the July 8, 1951, race at Bainbridge Fairgrounds (Ohio) while leading only the last lap of the race.

    TRUE   **FALSE**

59. The headlights on NASCAR race cars aren't actual headlights, but rather decals.

    TRUE   **FALSE**

60. The very first NASCAR premier series race at the Daytona Beach & Road Course on July 10, 1949, featured four female drivers.

    TRUE   **FALSE**

61. The drivers referenced in the previous question all appeared again in a race later that year on September 11, 1949, at Langhorne Speedway in Pennsylvania.

    TRUE   **FALSE**

62. The hill outside turns three and four of Phoenix International Raceway is known as "Rattlesnake Hill" because of all the rattlesnakes that populate the area.

   TRUE   FALSE

63. As of the beginning of the 2012 season, Casey Mears' sole victory in the NASCAR Sprint Cup Series came in the October 2007 race at Charlotte Motor Speedway.

   TRUE   FALSE

64. The multi-colored NASCAR bar logo has been used by the governing body since 1948.

   TRUE   FALSE

65. In a report released in 1973 in response to the Arab oil embargo, racing ranked behind basketball, football and other sports in oil use.

   TRUE   FALSE

66. The 1998 Daytona 500 was held on February 15, 50 years to the day after NASCAR ran its first race.

    TRUE   **FALSE**

67. Dale Earnhardt Jr. has been racing professionally since he was five years old.

    TRUE   **FALSE**

68. In 2011, Tony Stewart had the second fewest top-5 finishes of any NASCAR premier series champion since 1950.

    TRUE   **FALSE**

69. Jeff Gordon and his stepfather converted fairground land into a makeshift track in his hometown of Vallejo, California.

    TRUE   **FALSE**

70. On January 23, 2012, Danica Patrick announced that she would forego the 2012 Indy 500 in the IndyCar Series to compete in the Coca-Cola 600 in the NASCAR Sprint Cup Series.

TRUE   FALSE

71. As of the beginning of the 2012 season, Jack Roush had a total of 300 wins in NASCAR's three national series as an owner.

TRUE   FALSE

72. Louise Smith finished 30th in her final NASCAR premier series race on July 11, 1952, at Morristown Speedway (New Jersey).

TRUE   FALSE

73. Bill France Jr. was in attendance at the late-1947 meeting Bill France Sr. called in order to discuss the future of stock car racing.

TRUE   FALSE

74. Bill France Sr. was born and raised in Daytona Beach, Florida.

   TRUE   **FALSE**

75. In NASCAR's early days, young drivers sometimes raced using false names so their parents would not find out.

   TRUE   **FALSE**

76. Lee Petty's first racing garage was a converted chicken coop.

   TRUE   **FALSE**

77. Holman Moody's race shop used to reside on the land where the Time Warner Cable Arena, home of the NBA's Charlotte Bobcats, now sits.

   TRUE   **FALSE**

78. All NASCAR race cars are equipped with fire extinguishers.

   TRUE   **FALSE**

79. In 2003, to ensure the hoods and deck lids of race cars were more secure, NASCAR switched from steel tethers to ones made of Lexan, a stronger and more flexible product.

TRUE   FALSE

80. Roof flaps are primarily used on race cars to help the car continue in the right direction when it spins out.

TRUE   FALSE

81. The windshield of a NASCAR Sprint Cup Series race car has layers of adhesive film on it that pit crews can tear off during pit stops if scratches, bugs or other elements are limiting a driver's vision.

TRUE   FALSE

82. Drivers involved in minor accidents who have had to leave their cars are not required to visit the infield care center.

TRUE   FALSE

83. The NASCAR Nationwide Series has previously sanctioned events in both Canada and Mexico.

   TRUE   FALSE

84. During the 2012 NASCAR Sprint Cup Series season, NASCAR required electronic fuel injection in the race cars.

   TRUE   FALSE

85. The first NASCAR race to appear on television was the 1959 Daytona 500, which appeared on ABC's *Wide World of Sports*.

   TRUE   FALSE

86. The first NASCAR premier series race televised on ESPN was in 1982 at Charlotte Motor Speedway.

   TRUE   FALSE

87. Terry Labonte won two NASCAR premier series championships 12 years apart (1984 and 1996).

TRUE   FALSE

88. Jimmie Johnson ditched his No. 48 Chevrolet to pilot the No. 5 Chevrolet during the 2011 NASCAR Sprint All-Star Race.

TRUE   FALSE

89. Martin Truex Jr. won three straight NASCAR Nationwide Series championships from 2003 to 2005.

TRUE   FALSE

90. Brian Vickers only appeared in the first 11 races of the 2010 NASCAR Sprint Cup Series season before cutting his season short because of a blood-clotting condition.

TRUE   FALSE

91. As of the end of the 2011 NASCAR Nationwide Series season, no driver has claimed the championship more than twice.

TRUE   **FALSE**

92. All of the championships Dale Inman earned as a crew chief came while partnering with Richard Petty.

TRUE   **FALSE**

93. The largest points differential between a NASCAR premier series champion and the second-place finisher was in 1964, when Richard Petty finished 5,302 points ahead of second-place driver Ned Jarrett.

TRUE   **FALSE**

94. Darrell Waltrip won the very first NASCAR All-Star Race in 1985.

TRUE   **FALSE**

95. In 2008, Kasey Kahne won the NASCAR Sprint Fan Vote to compete in the NASCAR Sprint All-Star Race and went on to win that year's event at Charlotte Motor Speedway.

    TRUE   **FALSE**

96. Dale Earnhardt won the first Budweiser Shootout at Daytona.

    TRUE   **FALSE**

97. Cale Yarborough holds the all-time record in the Gatorade Duels with 12 victories.

    TRUE   **FALSE**

98. As of the beginning of the 2012 season, Jeff Gordon holds the qualifying record in the NASCAR Sprint Cup Series at Watkins Glen International.

    TRUE   **FALSE**

99. The farthest back in the starting field an eventual winner of the Daytona 500 has ever begun the Great American Race was in 2009, when Matt Kenseth started the race in the 39th position.

TRUE   FALSE

100. As of the beginning of the 2012 season, no NASCAR premier series driver has ever won the race at Homestead-Miami Speedway starting from the pole position.

TRUE   FALSE

101. Juan Pablo Montoya started from the 32nd position in the 2007 NASCAR Sprint Cup Series race at Sonoma and went on to win the race by a margin of just over four seconds.

TRUE   FALSE

102. Richard Petty has the most starts from the pole position in the NASCAR premier series with 123, while David Pearson is second with 113.

TRUE   FALSE

103. In 2007, 2008 and 2010, all three of the full-time NASCAR Sprint Cup Series drivers for Richard Childress Racing qualified for the Chase for the NASCAR Sprint Cup.

    TRUE   **FALSE**

104. During its tenure in the NASCAR Sprint Cup Series, Red Bull Racing never had a driver qualify for the Chase for the NASCAR Sprint Cup.

    TRUE   **FALSE**

105. The most combined NASCAR Sprint Cup Series wins the Joe Gibbs Racing drivers have had in one season was 10 in 2008 (Kyle Busch – 8, Tony Stewart – 1, Denny Hamlin – 1).

    TRUE   **FALSE**

106. As of the beginning of the 2012 NASCAR Sprint Cup Series season, Hendrick Motorsports was 1 win shy of 200 in the series over the team's long and storied career.

    TRUE   **FALSE**

107. Greg Biffle's first win in the NASCAR premier series came at Daytona International Speedway in 2003.

    TRUE   FALSE

108. Brothers Ward and Jeff Burton both drove race cars sponsored by Caterpillar at some point in their NASCAR premier series careers.

    TRUE   FALSE

109. In 1997, Jeff Burton won his first race in the NASCAR premier series at New Hampshire Motor Speedway.

    TRUE   FALSE

110. Kurt Busch was suspended by his car owner for the last three races of the 2005 NASCAR premier series season.

    TRUE   FALSE

111. Richard Petty did not race in the first Daytona 500 in 1959, which his father won after NASCAR officials spent three days consulting photos to determine the official winner.

     TRUE   FALSE

112. Race cars at Watkins Glen International run the track clockwise with pit road on the drivers' right side instead of their left.

     TRUE   FALSE

113. Indianapolis Motor Speedway is the world's oldest continually operating speedway.

     TRUE   FALSE

114. Bill France Sr. never competed in a race.

     TRUE   FALSE

115. Homestead-Miami Speedway was built in 1995 to help revitalize the surrounding communities that had been destroyed by Hurricane Andrew on August 24, 1992.

   TRUE   FALSE

116. Texas Motor Speedway presents the winner of the NASCAR Sprint Cup Series race with a cowboy hat and two pistols, along with a trophy.

   TRUE   FALSE

117. Lakewood Speedway in Georgia was originally built for horse racing.

   TRUE   FALSE

118. Turns 1 and 2 at North Wilkesboro Speedway are 15 feet lower than Turns 3 and 4 because the track was built on a sloped hill.

   TRUE   FALSE

119. There are no NASCAR-sanctioned race tracks in the greater New York City metro area.

TRUE   FALSE

120. When Jimmie Johnson and Chad Knaus claimed the NASCAR Sprint Cup Series championship in 2008 it marked the first time the same driver–crew chief team had won three consecutive titles in the series.

TRUE   FALSE

121. The catch can man is the member of the over-the-wall pit crew responsible for catching any overflow fuel during refueling.

TRUE   FALSE

122. The first time a race car is inspected is just prior to qualifying for a race.

TRUE   FALSE

123. When NASCAR officials find something illegal or questionable on a race car they cannot confiscate the part in question.

> **TRUE   FALSE**

124. Even though what is today called the NASCAR Nationwide Series only goes back to 1982, the series' roots can be traced back to 1950 and the NASCAR Sportsman Division.

> **TRUE   FALSE**

125. A current NASCAR Sprint Cup Series driver who finishes 43rd in a field of 43 cars and did not lead a lap during the race will only receive one point for the race.

> **TRUE   FALSE**

126. Drivers in each of the three national touring series are the only ones competing for points during a race weekend.

> **TRUE   FALSE**

127. NASCAR race teams often hire athletes from other sports for spots on a team's over-the-wall pit crew.

   TRUE   FALSE

128. Drivers who miss or are late for the mandatory pre-race driver/crew chief meeting must start at the back of the field.

   TRUE   FALSE

129. Since a NASCAR race car does not have a speedometer, drivers must rely on a tachometer, which measures an engine's rpm, when driving on pit road.

   TRUE   FALSE

130. Due to cooling systems positioned inside NASCAR race cars temperatures inside the cockpits rarely exceed 100 degrees.

   TRUE   FALSE

131. Two drivers won every NASCAR Modified Tour championship between 1971 and 1985.

    TRUE   FALSE

132. In 2010, NASCAR Sprint Cup Series driver Kyle Busch's team, Kyle Busch Motorsports, won the NASCAR Camping World Truck Series owners' championship in the team's inaugural season.

    TRUE   FALSE

133. David Gilliland played on his high-school golf team with PGA star Tiger Woods.

    TRUE   FALSE

134. Kevin Harvick married DeLana Linville on February 24, 2001, two days before he made his debut in the NASCAR premier series.

    TRUE   FALSE

135. Kevin Harvick filled in behind the steering wheel of the No. 3 GM Goodwrench Chevrolet in 2001 after Dale Earnhardt passed away earlier that season.

TRUE   FALSE

136. The GRAND-AM Rolex Sports Car Series has never visited the historic Indianapolis Motor Speedway to race.

TRUE   FALSE

137. TV and film star Patrick Dempsey owns a team and races in the GRAND-AM Rolex Sports Car Series GT class.

TRUE   FALSE

138. In 2009, Jimmie Johnson was named the Associated Press Male Athlete of the Year, the second race car driver to receive such distinction in 78 years of the award.

TRUE   FALSE

139. In 2004, only four NASCAR premier series drivers ranked in the top 10 in points after every race during the season: Dale Earnhardt Jr., Matt Kenseth, Elliott Sadler and Tony Stewart.

TRUE   FALSE

140. Brad Keselowski owns his own race team, fielding race trucks in the NASCAR Camping World Truck Series.

TRUE   FALSE

141. Travis Kvapil won his only pole in the NASCAR Sprint Cup Series at Bristol Motor Speedway.

TRUE   FALSE

142. In 2010, Bobby Labonte competed in the NASCAR Sprint Cup Series for four different owners/teams.

TRUE   FALSE

143. Mark Martin is the oldest race winner in the NASCAR premier series.

    TRUE   **FALSE**

144. Joey Logano is the youngest-ever winner of the Rookie of the Year in the NASCAR Sprint Cup Series.

    TRUE   **FALSE**

145. Jamie McMurray won the Daytona 500, Brickyard 400 and Bank of America 500 all in the same season: 2010.

    TRUE   **FALSE**

146. Earl Ross was the first foreign-born driver to have multiple wins in the NASCAR premier series.

    TRUE   **FALSE**

147. David Reutimann's first victory in the NASCAR Sprint Cup Series came at the Coca-Cola 600 at Charlotte Motor Speedway on May 24, 2009.

TRUE   FALSE

148. The first victory Stewart-Haas Racing had in NASCAR Sprint Cup Series competition came at the 2009 NASCAR Sprint All-Star Race.

TRUE   FALSE

149. Sam Hornish Jr. won the Indy 500 the year before he started racing full-time in the NASCAR Sprint Cup Series.

TRUE   FALSE

150. Five-time NASCAR Sprint Cup Series champion crew chief Chad Knaus served as a tire changer for Jeff Gordon's original pit crew in the NASCAR premier series.

TRUE   FALSE

ANSWER KEY
TRUE / FALSE

1. True.

2. False. NASCAR was incorporated on February 21, 1948.

3. False. NASCAR's headquarters are located in Daytona Beach, Florida.

4. True.

5. False. The 2010 and 2011 April Talladega races set the record for most lead changes at 88. The 2010 October Talladega race is right behind the record with 87 lead changes.

6. False. Alan Kulwicki won the championship as a driver-owner in the NASCAR premier series in 1992, the last time this feat was accomplished before Stewart won in 2011.

7. True.

8. True.

9. False. As of the end of the 2011 season, the No. 11 race car has a combined 231 wins between the three national series compared to 201 wins for the No. 43 race car.

10. False. Herb Thomas had 48 wins in 228 races for a win percentage of 21.05, while David Pearson had 105 wins in 574 wins for 18.29 percent.

11. True.

12. True.

13. False. When Tony Stewart won the season finale in his 2011 championship season it was the seventh time this had occurred in the NASCAR premier series. Other drivers to accomplish this feat were Tim Flock (1955), Buck Baker (1956 and 1957), Ned Jarrett (1965), Richard Petty (1971) and Jeff Gordon (1998).

14. True.

15. False. Joey Logano was unable to complete the Atomic Bomb Challenge at a restaurant near Watkins Glen, New York. The challenge consisted of eating a three-pound bacon cheeseburger loaded with pulled pork and a meaty sauce over a pound of fries in 30 minutes.

16. True.

17. False. In 2012, NASCAR began sanctioning the EURO-RACECAR as a NASCAR Touring Series in Europe on top of the two series already running in Canada and Mexico.

18. **False.** This is one year longer than Petty Enterprises' actual streak. They had at least one car win a race in the series every year between 1949 and 1977.

19. **True.**

20. **True.**

21. **False.** For a time, during the mid-1950s, it was against NASCAR rules to refuel a car during a caution period.

22. **False.** Maurice Petty made his NASCAR premier series driving debut at Dixie Speedway in Birmingham, Alabama, on August 3, 1960. He finished eighth out of 16 competitors. His driving career consisted of 26 starts, 7 top-5 and 16 top-10 finishes.

23. **False.** Joey Logano beat Kyle Busch's age record four years later when he won on June 28, 2009, at New Hampshire Motor Speedway in the Lenox Industrial Tools 301. Logano was 19 years, 1 month and 4 days old when he scored his first victory in the NASCAR Sprint Cup Series compared to Kyle Busch's age of 20 years, 4 months and 2 days.

24. **True.**

25. **False.** There were actually four Flock siblings who competed in

NASCAR races. Bob, Fonty and Tim Flock all raced in the NASCAR premier series, as did their sister, Ethel.

26. **False.** Indy cars competed on the historic track three times (1950, 1951 and 1956).

27. **True.**

28. **True.**

29. **False.** The first year every race on the NASCAR premier series schedule was televised live was actually 1989.

30. **False.** Harry Gant actually earned the nickname "Mr. September" after winning four consecutive NASCAR premier series races in September 1991 at the age of 51.

31. **False.** Richie Evans was awarded the 1985 championship in the NASCAR Modified Tour after dying as a result of an accident during a practice session prior to the last race of the season.

32. **True.**

33. **False.** Mike Stefanik won the NASCAR Modified Tour seven times and the NASCAR K&N Pro Series East twice, tying Richie Evans' nine titles.

34. True.

35. True.

36. False. Richard Petty was an offensive lineman on the Randleman High School football team, while his cousin Dale Inman was a halfback.

37. True.

38. False. The motorsports organization actually sanctions more than 1,200 races at around 100 tracks across more than 30 U.S. states, Canada and Mexico every year. In 2012, NASCAR also began sanctioning the EURO-RACECAR, which is a NASCAR Touring Series in Europe.

39. True.

40. False. The recycling program is actually the largest in all of sports. All tires, oils, fluids and batteries used in NASCAR races are recaptured and recycled.

41. False. Alan Kulwicki only had five career trips to Victory Lane in the NASCAR premier series, two of them coming in his championship season of 1992 and one win in 1988, 1990 and 1991.

42. False. Terry Labonte ended the 2011 season with 22 career wins in the NASCAR Sprint Cup Series while his younger brother Bobby was one back with 21.

43. True.

44. True.

45. False. Jeff Gordon holds the record with nine victories on road courses in the NASCAR Sprint Cup Series.

46. False. While Richard and Kyle Petty are two of the founders of Victory Junction, as well as being the Vice-Chairman and President respectively, Kyle's wife, Pattie, serves as the camp's Chairperson and CEO.

47. True.

48. False. Adam Sandler and Kevin James were at Michigan in 2010 to promote their movie, *Grown Ups.*

49. True.

50. True.

51. False. Jeff Gordon has appeared on the show in one or the other capacity at least 12 times.

52. **True.**

53. **False.** The track has 12 turns during NASCAR Sprint Cup Series events.

54. **True.**

55. **True.**

56. **True.**

57. **False.** The half-mile track is actually located in Willow Springs, Illinois, and is not the largest track in Illinois.

58. **False.** Flock led all 100 laps of the 100-mile event at the 1-mile dirt track.

59. **True.**

60. **False.** Three female drivers appeared in the first NASCAR premier series race at the famous track. They were Ethel Mobley, Sara Christian and Louise Smith.

61. **True.**

62. **True.**

63. **False.** Casey Mears did win at Charlotte Motor Speedway in 2007, but his victory came in the Coca-Cola 600 that May.

64. **False.** The NASCAR bar logo currently used by the governing body has only been around since 1976.

65. **True.**

66. **True.**

67. **False.** Dale Earnhardt Jr. has only been racing professionally since he was 17.

68. **True.**

69. **True.**

70. **True.**

71. **False.** By the end of the 2011 season, Jack Roush's team had only garnered 299 wins in NASCAR's three national series.

72. **True.**

73. **False.** At the time of the meeting, Bill France Jr. would have been a teenager and not involved in the initial meetings.

74. False. Bill France was born in Washington, D.C., in 1909 and moved to Daytona Beach, Florida, in the 1930s.

75. True.

76. True.

77. False. Holman Moody's race shop was located on part of the land where the Charlotte Douglas International Airport is today.

78. True.

79. False. The material for the new tethers NASCAR introduced in 2003 was Vectran.

80. False. Roof flaps are used primarily to help prevent spinning race cars from becoming airborne.

81. True.

82. False. All drivers involved in any type of accident that causes them to stop driving must be checked out by a medical professional at the infield care center, even if they feel fine.

83. True.

TRUE–FALSE ANSWER KEY

84. **True.**

85. **False.** The first race *Wide World of Sports* televised, although not live, was the July 4, 1961, race at Daytona International Speedway. Additionally, on January 31, 1960, CBS broadcast the NASCAR premier series qualifying races for the Daytona 500 live on *CBS Sports Spectacular*.

86. **False.** ESPN's first televised NASCAR event was a 1981 race that was run at Atlanta Motor Speedway.

87. **True.**

88. **True.**

89. **False.** Martin Truex Jr. won two consecutive NASCAR Nationwide Series championships in 2004 and 2005. Brian Vickers won the championship in 2003.

90. **True.**

91. **True.**

92. **False.** Dale Inman earned seven championships as a crew chief while working with Richard Petty, but he also earned one with Terry Labonte in 1984.

93. False. The largest points differential was in 1967 when Richard Petty finished 6,028 points ahead of James Hylton.

94. True.

95. True.

96. False. The first Budweiser Shootout was in 1979 and was won by Buddy Baker. Dale Earnhardt won the event in 1980.

97. False. Cale Yarborough is in second place with six Gatorade Duel wins, while Dale Earnhardt has 12 victories.

98. False. As of the beginning of the 2012 season, the record belongs to Kyle Busch, who set a new qualifying benchmark for the 2011 Watkins Glen race putting down a lap of 126.421 mph.

99. True.

100. False. It has happened twice. Bill Elliott won at Homestead-Miami Speedway from the pole in 2001 and Kurt Busch did the same thing the following year.

101. True.

102. True.

103. True.

104. False. In 2009, Brian Vickers made the Chase for the NASCAR Sprint Cup and finished 12th in the final points standings.

105. False. In 2010, Denny Hamlin had 8 wins while Kyle Busch had 3 to set the record for most combined wins in a season by a Joe Gibbs Racing stable of drivers at 11.

106. True.

107. True.

108. True.

109. False. Although Jeff Burton did win at New Hampshire in 1997, his first victory came 11 races earlier at Texas Motor Speedway.

110. False. Kurt Busch was suspended for only the last two races of the 2005 season by Jack Roush. Busch then signed with Roger Penske to drive for Penske Racing from 2006 until he was released after the 2011 season.

111. False. Richard Petty appeared in the inaugural event at the

Daytona International Speedway completing only 8 of the 200 laps and finishing 57th out of 59 drivers.

112. True.

113. False. This distinction actually belongs to The Milwaukee Mile (Wisconsin), which has hosted motorsports events since 1903. Although the track is still hosting events, the last NASCAR-sanctioned race the track ran was in 2009.

114. False. Bill France Sr. appeared in only one NASCAR-sanctioned race. It was held at Martinsville Speedway (Virginia) in 1948, a year before the NASCAR premier series was established. He finished fifth in the race and took no points or money. France signed up to enter the 1969 race at Talladega, but did not compete.

115. True.

116. True.

117. True.

118. True.

119. False. Riverhead Raceway, located on Long Island, opened in 1952 and has hosted NASCAR Modified Tour events for years.

120. True.

121. False. The position of the catch can man was eliminated prior to the start of the 2011 season when teams started using self-venting gas cans that prevent spills.

122. False. The chassis is inspected before the car is built and radio frequency identification (RFID) chips are attached. When the chassis goes through inspection at a track prior to a race, the NASCAR officials on track can use the RFIDs to verify that the chassis was previously approved.

123. False. NASCAR officials can, and often do, confiscate illegal or questionable parts they find on a race car.

124. True.

125. True.

126. False. Owners and car manufacturers also compete for championships every year.

127. True.

128. True.

129. True.

130. False. The drivers have cooling devices in their helmets and uniforms that help cool them off, but the temperature inside a race car can still hit 130 degrees.

131. True.

132. True.

133. True.

134. False. Kevin Harvick made his NASCAR premier series debut on February 26, 2001, at Rockingham Speedway, and he and DeLana Linville married two days later.

135. False. Kevin Harvick filled in for Dale Earnhardt in 2001, but Earnhardt's longstanding sponsor on the No. 3 Chevrolet transferred its sponsorship to the No. 29 Chevrolet piloted by Harvick.

136. False. The GRAND-AM Rolex Sports Car Series made its first visit to Indianapolis Motor Speedway on July 27, 2012, as part of the inaugural Super Weekend at The Brickyard, which also features a NASCAR Sprint Cup Series event.

137. **True.**

138. **False.** Jimmie Johnson was actually the first race car driver to receive the award, making it even more of an honor for Johnson.

139. **True.**

140. **True.**

141. **False.** Travis Kvapil earned his one pole in the NASCAR Sprint Cup Series at Talladega Superspeedway in 2008.

142. **True.**

143. **False.** Harry Gant holds that distinction, having won in the NASCAR premier series on August 16, 1992, at Michigan International Speedway when he was 52 years, 7 months and 6 days old.

144. **True.**

145. **True.**

146. **False.** As of the end of the 2011 season, Juan Pablo Montoya is the only foreign-born NASCAR premier series driver to win

at least two races (2007 and 2010). Canadian Earl Ross won only one race in the series, in 1974.

147. True.

148. True.

149. False. Sam Hornish Jr. won the Indy 500 in 2006, but did not start racing full-time in the NASCAR premier series until 2008.

150. True.

FILL IN THE BLANK

1. The slang term for the best route around a race track is

_____.

2. The horsepower for an engine in a NASCAR Nationwide Series car is _____.

3. The _____ in Daytona Beach, Florida, is where Bill France Sr. organized a meeting on December 14, 1947, to discuss the future of stock car racing.

4. A car is _____ if the front wheels lose traction before the rear wheels do.

5. The turbulent air currents caused by fast-moving cars is called

_____.

6. The air pressure traveling over the surfaces of a car creates
_____, or weight, on that area.

7. When a car isn't oversteering or understeering, but travels
around the race track as if it is on rails it is said to be in
_____.

8. _____ is the study of airflow and the forces of resistance
and pressure that result from the flow of air over, under and
around a moving car.

9. The amount a tire is tilted in or out from vertical, described in
degrees, is known as _____.

10. A _____ is a thin material, made of paper, metal, silicone
or other synthetic material, used as a seal between two similar
machined metal surfaces, such as cylinder heads and the
engine block.

11. Cars that have completed at least one full lap less than the race leader are known as _____.

.

12. Each time a tire is raised to operating temperature it is known as a _____.

13. An iron casting from the manufacturer that envelops the crank shaft, connecting rods and pistons is called an _____.

14. _____ is a slang term for black, circular, dent-line marks on the side panels of stock cars, usually caused by rubbing against other cars at a high speed.

15. The removable metal scoop at the base of the windshield and rear of the hood that directs air into the air box is called a _____.

16. _____ refers to the cross-weight adjustment on a race car.

17. A steel tube that connects the transmission of a race car to the rear-end housing is called a _____.

18. _____ is a measurement of mechanical or engine power that is calculated in the amount of power it takes to move 33,000 pounds one foot in one minute.

19. The sheet metal on both sides of the car from the C-post to the rear bumper below the deck lid and above the wheel well is called the _____.

20. A _____ is a valve in the wheel used to reduce air pressure on tires.

21. A _____ is a penalty usually assessed for speeding on the pit road or for unsafe driving. The car must be brought onto the pit road at the appropriate speed and stopped for one full second in the team's pit stall before returning to the track.

22. _____ are tires that have been used at least once and saved for further racing. They are most often used in qualifying.

23. Another term for the trunk lid of a race car is the _____.

24. The distance or time between two cars, referred to in car lengths or seconds, is an _____.

25. A _____ is a maneuver in which a car following the leader in a draft suddenly steers around it, breaking the vacuum to provide an extra burst of speed that allows the second car to take the lead.

26. A _____ is an overheating of the tread compound resulting in bubbles on the tire surface.

27. A _____ is an element used to reduce vibrations in the crank shaft, located on the front of an engine.

28. The difference in size between the tires on the left and right sides of a race car is known as _____. Because of a tire's makeup, slight variations in circumference result.

29. _____ is duct tape that is so strong it will hold a damaged race car together long enough to finish a race.

30. A _____ is a solid metal plate separating the engine compartment from the driver's cockpit of a race car.

31. _____ describes the turning or adjusting of a car's jacking screws found at each wheel.

32. _____ is the distance between the car's frame rails and the ground.

33. _____ is the condition when the inner liner of a tire loses air pressure, causing both the liner and outer tire to have the same pressure, creating a vibration.

34. _____ presented the first live flag-to-flag coverage of the Daytona 500 on February 18, 1979.

35. In 1959, _____ got its first major NASCAR win with Jim Reed's victory in the Southern 500 at Darlington Raceway.

36. _____ sponsored Kyle Busch's No. 99 Jack Roush–owned Ford truck for six races during the 2001 NASCAR Camping World Truck Series season.

37. The _____ is the nickname of Greg Biffle's No. 16 pit crew in the NASCAR Sprint Cup Series.

38. In the early 1960s, Ned Jarrett enrolled in a _____ course that focused on self-improvement and public speaking.

39. _____ sponsored Dale Earnhardt Jr.'s No. 3 Chevrolet that he drove to seven victories in 1998 in what is now the NASCAR Nationwide Series, winning his first of two consecutive championships in the series.

40. _____, which is a game on Facebook, is officially licensed by NASCAR.

41. _____ Program, implemented by NASCAR, plants 10 trees for each green flag that waves during a lot of NASCAR-sanctioned races. The trees capture 100 percent of the carbon produced by the on-track racing at the events.

42. The _____ is the 24-hour race that kicks off the start of the GRAND-AM Rolex Sports Car Series season and has featured such drivers as Jimmie Johnson, Juan Pablo Montoya, AJ Allmendinger and Danica Patrick, among others.

43. The paved portion of a race track separating the track from the infield is commonly referred to as the _____.

44. The end of a race where the final scheduled lap is run under caution, causing the race to be extended a few more laps to try to ensure the race ends under green, is called a _____ finish.

45. The number of attempts at ending the race in the manner that is explained in question 44 before NASCAR will call the race is

_____.

46. _____ is the NASCAR industry's leading development program for minority and female drivers and crew members.

47. The _____ owned Jeff Burton's No. 8 Ford that he raced in 1994 when he earned the NASCAR premier series Rookie of the Year.

48. _____ became the master toy licensee for NASCAR Team Properties in 2011 with products launching in 2012.

49. _____ is the annual charitable celebration that takes place every May and unifies the NASCAR community to better the lives of children.

50. _____ was a 2010 TV docu-series on BET featuring aspiring NASCAR drivers vying for a seat with Revolution Racing in the NASCAR K&N Pro Series and NASCAR Whelen All-American Series.

51. In October 2010, Sunoco and NASCAR announced that all race cars in the three national series would race with _____ fuel in their fuel cells.

52. _____ is often referred to as "The World's Fastest Half-Mile."

53. The _____ is a school located in Mooresville, North Carolina, that offers an intensive program in which students can learn the tools of the trade needed to become a technician in the NASCAR industry.

54. The _____ is the woven mesh that hangs across the driver's side window to prevent the driver's head and limbs from being exposed during an accident.

55. NASCAR celebrated its 60th anniversary in _____.

56. Joey Logano and Carl Edwards appeared on Cartoon Network's _____ in the summer of 2010 to advise teams competing against each other on how to blow up a race car.

57. The _____ is the distance between the axles on the same side of the car.

58. The _____ is the steel frame of the car.

59. Race tracks between one and two miles in length are considered

_____.

60. _____ are applied to wheels with a high-pressure air wrench during a pit stop to secure the tires in place.

61. A car's _____ is the slang term for the tuning and adjustments made to a race car's suspension before and during a race.

62. _____ is the term used to describe aggressive driving involving a lot of bumping and rubbing.

63. The foremost position on the starting grid that is awarded to the fastest qualifier is the _____.

64. _____ is the term used when referring to how a driver's race car is doing when it is neither pulling nor tight.

65. _____ is the term used to refer to the resistance a car experiences when passing through air at high speeds.

66. The _____ is the housing that directs the air-fuel mixture through the port openings in the cylinder heads.

67. The _____ is a lateral bar that connects the frame of a car to the rear axle, which keeps the rear tires centered within the body of the car.

68. _____ is another term for a race car's brakes.

69. A _____ is a quick pit stop that involves nothing more than refueling the race car with only the amount necessary to finish the race.

70. A _____ is a special formula or recipe of rubber used in a particular tire.

71. _____ is used to describe any patching material used to fill cracks and holes or smooth out bumps on a track's surface.

72. The weight, at a given tire position, put on a car due to aerodynamics, vehicle weight and lateral G-forces in a turn is called _____.

73. The _____ is a line painted on the track, near the apron and extending from the pit road exit into the first turn, which a driver leaving the pits needs to stay below in order to safely blend back into traffic.

74. _____ are devices used to check the race car's body shape and size to ensure compliance with NASCAR's guidelines.

75. The _____ is a cover surrounding the flywheel and clutch that connects the engine to the transmission.

76. A _____ is a holding tank, consisting of a metal box containing a flexible, tear-resistant bladder and foam baffling, used for a race car's supply of gasoline.

77. The _____ flag is the most famous one in motorsports, waving when the race leader crosses the finish line and a winner is determined.

78. The Martinsville _____ is considered one of the most famous concession-stand foods in NASCAR.

79. _____ was the popular advertising slogan car manufacturers used in the sport's early days to promote the fact that the cars raced on tracks were the same ones fans could buy at car dealerships.

80. In an attempt to challenge the 1969 Ford Cyclone and the 1969 Ford Torino Talladega, which had sloped noses that provided a distinctive advantage on track, Chrysler developed the 1969 Dodge _____ and 1970 Plymouth _____.

81. To gain an introduction to stock car racing, Jeff Gordon attended the _____ Driving School in North Carolina.

82. Because of his promotional expertise, Bill Tuthill was invited by Bill France to chair the meetings that led to NASCAR's creation in late 1947. He was later named NASCAR's first _____.

83. Rockingham Speedway is often referred to as _____.

84. Dover International Speedway's track is paved with _____.

85. _____ was used to pave Darlington Raceway, as well as a majority of the tracks running NASCAR Sprint Cup Series events.

86. The HANS device stands for _____.

87. _____ is a heat- and flame-resistant material developed by DuPont and used in drivers' uniforms to protect them from fire hazards.

88. SAFER barriers debuted in 2002 and were installed at oval tracks on the NASCAR Sprint Cup Series schedule. SAFER stands for _____.

89. None of the race cars in the NASCAR Sprint Cup Series have glass windshields; instead, they are made out of _____.

90. When the NASCAR Camping World Truck Series was first introduced in 1995 it was called the _____.

91. A _____ is waved when a driver is being told to head to pit road because they either violated a rule or need further inspection.

92. A _____ is waved when a driver ignores NASCAR's order to report to pit road. All laps they run under this flag will not be scored.

93. A _____ is waved when a slow driver is being ordered to yield to an approaching faster driver.

94. When looking at a race car from the front, the amount the tires are turned in or out is referred to as _____.

95. The _____ is used to resist or counteract the rolling force of the car's body through the turns.

96. A _____ is a metal blade attached to the rear deck lid of a race car in order to restrict airflow over the rear of the car, providing downforce and traction.

97. The steel tubing inside a race car designed to protect the driver from impacts or rollover is called a _____.

98. The _____ is a heavy metal rotating wheel that is part of the race car's clutch system used to keep parts like the crank shaft turning steadily.

99. _____ is a slang term used to describe racing a car as fast as possible under the given weather and track conditions.

100. _____ are the layers of fabric within a tire that are woven in angles, or tires that are made in this manner.

101. _____ race shop is located in Denver, Colorado. Most other race teams have their race shops in or around Charlotte, North Carolina.

102. _____ was named the 1980 Daytona 500 Rookie of the Year.

103. Neil Bonnett became a television commentator and hosted his own race show on _____.

104. Thomas Wolfe wrote an article that appeared in _____ magazine tabbing Junior Johnson as "The Last American Hero."

105. Glen Wood's nickname, which reflects of his life before NASCAR, is _____.

106. Tony Stewart appeared in a 2012 episode of _____, starring Tim Allen.

107. _____ has the most NASCAR premier series championships as a crew chief.

108. _____ sponsored Tony Stewart's race car when he first started competing in the NASCAR premier series.

109. A _____ is a reflective pad that provides extra protection for the driver's heel, which is always in contact with the hot floorboard of the race car.

110. _____ sponsored Kurt Busch's Jack Roush–owned No. 97 Ford during the 2000 NASCAR premier season, Busch's first year in the series.

111. When Darrell Waltrip won his first championship in the NASCAR premier series in 1981, his No. 11 Buick was sponsored by _____.

112. Michael Waltrip drove the _____ to victory in the 2001 Daytona 500 as a driver for DEI.

113. _____ is a former NBA player and current ESPN analyst who is a co-owner of JTG/Daugherty Racing.

114. Greg Biffle piloted the No. 16 _____-sponsored Ford for Jack Roush when he won his first race in the NASCAR premier series.

115. Tony Stewart purchased _____ in Rossburg, Ohio, in November 2004 and holds a Prelude to the Dream charity event there every year featuring stars from the NASCAR Sprint Cup Series.

116. In January 2012, NASCAR and _____ restructured their digital partnership, which provides NASCAR control over the business and editorial operations for its digital platforms beginning in 2013.

117. After winning a race, Alan Kulwicki's unique celebration where he drove around the track in the opposite direction was called a _____.

118. The _____ is what race cars earn when they scrape against the outside wall of the "Track Too Tough to Tame."

119. Hickory Motor Speedway is known as the _____ because of the many NASCAR stars who got their starts there.

120. Martinsville Speedway is nicknamed the _____ because of the shape of its track.

121. _____ are the members of a race team who shape sheet metal into the body of a race car.

122. The machine that race teams use to measure an engine's horsepower is called a _____.

123. The _____ is a rig that race teams use to transport two race cars, engines, tools and support equipment to races. They often act as a meeting space and/or locker room for the race team.

124. Prior to becoming a NASCAR team owner, Joe Gibbs coached the _____ to three Super Bowl championships – 1983, 1988 and 1992.

125. A _____ is the cart that teams have in their pit stalls with reserved spots for each piece of equipment and tools. The crew chief and other selected members of a race team sit atop it during races.

126. _____ sit above the grandstand and act as an extra set of eyes for drivers by providing direction to successfully navigate through accidents and avoid debris.

127. _____ has sponsored Denny Hamlin since he first appeared in seven races in the 2005 NASCAR Sprint Cup Series season.

128. As of the end of the 2011 season, _____ different drivers have won at least one race in the NASCAR premier series.

129. _____ was the long-term (1999–2009) sponsor of Matt Kenseth's Jack Roush–owned No. 17 Ford.

130. _____ sponsored the James Finch–owned No. 09 Chevrolet that Brad Keselowski drove to his first victory in the NASCAR Sprint Cup Series at Talladega Superspeedway on April 26, 2009.

131. When Terry Labonte won his first NASCAR premier series championship in 1984, _____ sponsored his Billy Hagan–owned No. 44 Chevrolet.

132. _____ was the longstanding sponsor of Richard Petty's No. 43 car. The company still has a partnership deal with Petty's team today.

133. Juan Pablo Montoya's charity, _____, benefits needy children in Colombia and the United States.

134. Darrell Waltrip's popular nickname, given to him by Cale Yarborough, is _____.

135. As of the end of the 2011 season, Ryan Newman had won _____ poles between NASCAR's three national touring series.

136. The _____ was a creative idea that Jack Roush's team used in 2005 to audition aspiring drivers for a seat in one of Roush's NASCAR Camping World Truck Series rides.

137. In 2010, Martin Truex Jr. won the _____ to qualify for that year's NASCAR Sprint All-Star Race.

138. _____ is the slogan for the Martin Truex Jr. Foundation, which raises funds for community programs and initiatives.

139. _____ was Bill Elliott's primary sponsor on his No. 9 Ford that he raced to the 1988 NASCAR premier series championship.

140. The _____ extends from the roofline to the base of the windshield on either side of the car.

141. A _____ is part of the braking system that, when applied by the driver, clamps the brake disk/rotor to slow or stop the car.

142. A _____ is a race track straightaway.

143. _____ is the practice of two or more cars running nose-to-tail while racing. The lead car, by displacing the air in front of it, creates a vacuum between its rear end and the nose of the following car, actually pulling the second car along with it.

144. _____ is short for "magnetic particle inspection," which is a procedure for checking all steel parts (suspension pieces, connecting rods, cylinder heads) for cracks and other defects utilizing a solution of metal particles, fluorescent dye and a black light. Surface cracks appear as red lines under this light.

145. The area along the pit road that is designated for a particular team's use during pit stops is called a _____.

146. The _____ is presented to the eligible driver who gains the most positions from his or her starting to finishing position in each event.

147. The _____ is awarded to the crew chief of the driver who improves the most from the first half of the race to the second half of the race utilizing the 40 best lap times.

148. The _____ goes to the eligible driver who records the fastest average speed on restarts and finishes the race on the lead lap.

149. The _____ is awarded to the crew chief of the driver who has demonstrated the best qualifying and race effort based on finishing positions during the weekend.

150. The _____ is presented to the eligible driver who leads the most laps in an event.

1. **Groove**

2. **650 at 8,200 RPM**

3. **Streamline Hotel**

4. **Tight**

5. **Dirty Air**

6. **Downforce**

7. **Balance**

8. **Aerodynamics**

9. **Camber**

10. **Gasket**

11. **Lapped Traffic**

12. **Heat Cycle**

13. **Engine Block**

14. **Donuts**

15. **Cowl**

16. **Wedge**

17. **Drive Shaft**

18. **Horsepower**

19. **Quarter Panel**

20. **Bleeder Valve**

21. **Stop and Go**

22. **Scuffs**

23. **Deck Lid**

24. **Interval**

25. **Slingshot**

26. **Blister**

27. **Harmonic Balancer**

28. **Stagger**

29. **Racer's Tape or 200-mph Tape**

30. **Firewall**

31. **Round of Bite**

32. **Ride Height**

33. **Equalized**

34. **CBS Sports**

35. **Goodyear Tire & Rubber Company**

36. **Eldon**

37. **Pit Bulls**

38. **Dale Carnegie**

39. **AC Delco**

40. **Car Town**

41. **NASCAR Green Clean Air**

42. **Rolex 24 At Daytona**

43. **Apron**

44. **Green-white-checkered**

45. **Three**

46. **Drive for Diversity**

47. **Stavola Brothers**

48. **Spin Master**

49. **NASCAR Day**

50. *Changing Lanes*

51. **Sunoco Green E15**

52. **Bristol Motor Speedway**

53. **NASCAR Technical Institute**

54. **Window Net**

55. **2008**

56. *Destroy Build Destroy*

57. **Wheelbase**

58. **Chassis**

59. **Intermediate Tracks**

60. **Lug Nuts**

61. **Setup**

62. **Trading Paint**

63. **Pole Position**

64. **Neutral**

65. **Drag**

66. **Intake Manifold**

67. **Track Bar**

68. **Binders**

69. **Splash and Go**

70. **Compound**

71. **Bear Grease**

72. **Loading**

73. **Blend Line**

74. **Templates**

75. **Bell Housing**

76. **Fuel Cell**

77. **Checkered**

78. **Hot Dog**

79. **"Win on Sunday, Sell on Monday"**

80. **Daytona; Superbird**

81. **Buck Baker**

82. **Executive Secretary**

83. **"The Rock"**

84. **Concrete**

85. **Asphalt**

86. **Head and Neck Support**

87. **Nomex**

88. **Steel and Foam Energy Reduction**

89. **Lexan**

90. **NASCAR Craftsman SuperTruck Series**

91. **Black Flag**

92. **Black Flag with a White X**

93. **Blue Flag with Diagonal Stripes**

94. **Toe**

95. **Sway Bar**

96. **Spoiler**

97. **Roll Cage**

98. **Flywheel**

99. **Flat-Out**

100. **Bias-Ply**

101. **Furniture Row Racing's**

102. **Tim Richmond**

103. **The Nashville Network**

104. *Esquire*

105. **The Woodchipper**

106. *Last Man Standing*

107. **Dale Inman**

108. **The Home Depot**

109. **Heel Shield**

110. **John Deere**

111. **Mountain Dew**

112. **No. 15 NAPA Chevrolet**

113. **Brad Daugherty**

114. **Grainger**

115. **Eldora Speedway**

116. **Turner Sports**

117. **Polish Victory Lap**

118. **Darlington Stripe**

119. **"Birthplace of the NASCAR Stars"**

120. **"Paperclip"**

121. **Fabricators**

122. **Dynamometer**

123. **Hauler or Transporter**

124. **Washington Redskins**

125. **War Wagon**

126. **Spotters**

127. **FedEx**

128. **182**

129. **DeWalt**

130. **Miccosukee Resorts & Gaming**

131. Piedmont Airlines

132. STP

133. Formula Smiles Foundation

134. "Jaws"

135. 62

136. Gong Show

137. Sprint Showdown

138. "Hooked on Helping"

139. Coors

140. A-Post

141. Brake Caliper

142. Chute

143. Drafting

NASCAR TRIVIA

1. Prior to becoming a successful driver in the NASCAR Sprint Cup Series, Carl Edwards passed out business cards that touted his driving skills.

2. Looking to promote their product, Heinz 57, Heinz sponsored Rod Osterlund's No. 57 car in 1990, which was driven by Jimmy Spencer.

3. When Dale Earnhardt raced in the Pepsi 400 at Michigan International Speedway in 2000 along with his sons, Kerry and Dale Jr., it was the second time a father and two sons ran in the same NASCAR premier series event.

4. As of the beginning of the 2012 season, 9 of the top-10 most competitive races (ones with the most different leaders) in the NASCAR Sprint Cup Series were held at Talladega Superspeedway.

5. Dale Earnhardt won an incredible 34 races at Daytona International Speedway, a track record. He has won NASCAR Sprint Cup Series points races, NASCAR Nationwide Series races, Budweiser Shootouts, Gatorade Duels and IROC races at the track. The closest driver is Tony Stewart with 17 victories.

6. On July 16, 2011, Kyle Busch won the NASCAR Nationwide Series race at New Hampshire Motor Speedway, leading 33 of the 206 laps. The victory gave Busch 100 total combined victories between the three national touring series. By the end of the 2011

season, Busch would make 4 more trips to Victory Lane in the three series for a total of 104 wins between the series during his relatively short career (23 wins in the NASCAR Sprint Cup Series, 51 wins in the NASCAR Nationwide Series and 30 wins in the NASCAR Camping World Truck Series).

7. Mamie Reynolds, at 19 years old, became the first female – as well as the youngest – car owner to win in the NASCAR premier series. The race was held on September 13, 1962, and Fred Lorenzen drove the Reynolds-owned car to the checkered flag at Augusta Speedway in Georgia.

8. The second-to-last race of the 1956 season was held on November 11 at Hickory Speedway in North Carolina, the same day the first race of the 1957 season was held at Willow Springs Speedway in Lancaster, California.

9. There have been several times in the history of the NASCAR premier series that two races have been run on the same day, but on October 14, 1951, and May 21, 1961, the NASCAR premier series held three races.

10. The Daytona 500 didn't become the official, permanent start to the NASCAR premier series until 1982, when Bobby Allison won the Great American Race.

11. Tim Richmond's No. 2 Buick featured a mock sponsorship from Clyde Torkle's Chicken Pit Special in the 1982 World 600 at Charlotte Motor Speedway to promote the movie *Stroker Ace*.

12. Jeff Gordon's first race in the NASCAR Sprint Cup Series was on November 15, 1992, at Atlanta Motor Speedway. The race was Richard Petty's very last race in the series. Gordon finished 31st, while Petty finished 35th in the race won by Bill Elliott.

13. Walt Disney World Speedway, located on the grounds of Walt Disney World in Orlando, Florida, hosted NASCAR Camping World Truck Series races in 1997 and 1998.

14. According to Bones Bourcier's book, *Richie!: The Fast Life and Times of NASCAR's Greatest Modified Driver*, Richie Evans won an estimated 477 wins in the NASCAR Modified Tour.

15. Tony Stewart raced in both the Indianapolis 500 and the Coca-Cola 600 on May 30, 1999. He had top-10 finishes in both races, finishing ninth and fourth, respectively.

16. Tony Stewart and Carl Edwards tied in the final points standings at the end of the 2011 season, the closest finish in NASCAR history. The tiebreaker went to Stewart, who had five victories versus Edwards' one.

17. On February 9, 1952, Al Stevens carried a two-way radio in his race car during the NASCAR Modified Sportsman event on the Daytona Beach & Road Course, the first time two-way radio communication was used in the sport.

18. Clint Bowyer was working at a fabrication shop in his hometown of Emporia, Kansas, when Richard Childress called to inquire about hiring him as a driver. Bowyer almost didn't take the call thinking one of his friends was playing a joke on him.

19. The No. 42, No. 48 and No. 88 race cars usually driven by Juan Pablo Montoya, Jimmie Johnson and Dale Earnhardt Jr., respectively, in the NASCAR Sprint Cup Series appeared as Transformers in the 2011 blockbuster movie, *Transformers: Dark of the Moon.*

20. Dale Earnhardt Jr. won the Daytona 500 on February 15, 2004, six years to the day after his father won it.

21. In 2008, famed artist Thomas Kinkade was licensed by NASCAR to paint the 50th running of the Daytona 500. In 2011, Kinkade released his second NASCAR-licensed piece. The newer work featured Talladega Superspeedway and the No. 3 race car of the late Dale Earnhardt.

22. On July 4, 1984, Ronald Reagan became the first sitting U.S.

president to attend a NASCAR premier series race. He gave the signal "Gentlemen, start your engines!" from aboard Air Force One, which was parked at the airport adjacent to Daytona International Speedway. Richard Petty went on to win the 200th and final victory of his illustrious career that day.

23. Junior Johnson can be credited for helping bring R.J. Reynolds Tobacco and their Winston brand of cigarettes to NASCAR. R.J. Reynolds was interested in sponsoring Johnson's car, but had more budget to work with than what it cost. Johnson suggested they consider talking to NASCAR about sponsoring the whole series instead, and Winston ended up the title sponsor for NASCAR's premier series.

24. Tim Flock drove with a rhesus monkey in his race car for eight races during the 1953 season. On May 16, Flock won the NASCAR premier series race at Hickory Motor Speedway (North Carolina) with the monkey, Jocko Flocko, riding shotgun. Flock retired Jocko Flocko a couple weeks later when, during the Raleigh 300 at Raleigh Speedway (North Carolina), the monkey got freaked out when he stuck his head through the trap door on the floorboard. Flock is the only driver in NASCAR history to pit in order to remove a monkey from his car.

25. In 1951, the states of North Carolina, New Jersey and California proposed bills to "prohibit and curtail all forms of auto racing."

Bill France was instrumental in addressing the threat and the Congressional bill never made it to the floor.

26. On the 90th lap of the 1973 Talladega 500, driver Bobby Isaac suddenly pulled his Bud Moore–owned Ford into the pits and got out of the car. Isaac told Moore that a voice told him to quit driving. Isaac retired right then and Coo Coo Marlin took over driving responsibilities for the rest of the race. Although that was Issac's last race of the 1973 season, he appeared in 19 races in the NASCAR premier series over the next three years.

27. NASCAR premier series driver George Seeger of Whittier, California, drove his Tony Sampo–owned Studebaker to a 20th-place finish in the 1951 Southern 500 at Darlington Raceway in South Carolina. During Seeger's trip home with Sampo, they got into an argument while stopped at a gas station in Phoenix, Arizona. Sampo drove off when Seeger got out to use the restroom, leaving him stranded without any transportation home.

28. Jimmy Florian drove to victory at Dayton Speedway in Ohio on June 25, 1950, without a shirt. He later said that he removed it because he was unusually hot and there was nothing in the NASCAR rule book that stated a driver was required to wear a shirt during a race.

29. On September 28, 1952, Herb Thomas won the 100 Miles race at Wilson Speedway in North Carolina with an average speed of 35.398 mph. It holds the record for the slowest race in the NASCAR premier series.

30. Junior Johnson built up such a lead in the 1961 Virginia 500 at the Martinsville Speedway in Virginia that his crew repeatedly gave him the "EZ" sign to slow him down. During one of his pit stops, Johnson was threatened with a sledgehammer by Rex Lovette, his car owner, who demanded he slow down and save the car.

31. On February 9, 1952, Al Stevens placed 27th out of 118 cars in a NASCAR Modified Sportsman Division race at the Daytona Beach & Road Course. Alongside him in his car was a government-surplus phone from WWII that sat on a big box. Using the phone, he was able to communicate with his owner/crew chief, Cotton Bennett, and two spotters who helped him successfully navigate around a couple of accidents during the race.

32. Joe Frasson was fined $100 by NASCAR for beating his car with a jack handle. He was frustrated with his Pontiac after he failed to qualify for the 1975 World 600 in Charlotte, North Carolina. Frasson later qualified for the race driving Henley Gray's No. 19 Chevrolet.

33. A driver named J. Christopher from New York City drove a Jaguar in the 100-mile event at Linden Airport on June 13, 1954. Christopher had to drop out of the race after only 23 laps because of mechanical problems, finishing 39th. Christopher raced with an amateur sports-car group and changed his name for the Linden Airport event to protect his amateur standing. His real name was Conrad Janis, and he was a famous jazz musician and actor who played Mindy's father on the 1970s TV show *Mork and Mindy*.

34. Tiny Lund won the 1963 Daytona 500 on only one set of tires. His pit crew, the famous Wood Brothers – known for their lightning-fast pit stops – did not have to change a single tire all day.

35. On April 12, 1952, an "overserved" race fan attempted to drive across the track during the NASCAR premier series race at Columbia Speedway in South Carolina. A Ford driven by E.C. Ramsey could not avoid the car and plowed into it, eliminating Ramsey from the event. Ramsey was unharmed in the accident.

36. Racing pioneer Joe Littlejohn installed a special seat in Herb Thomas' Hudson and rode with Thomas as a passenger during qualifying for the 100-mile event at Asheville-Weaverville Speedway in North Carolina. Thomas set a qualifying record that day with Littlejohn as co-pilot.

37. In the inaugural World 600 at Charlotte Motor Speedway on June 19, 1960, Jack Smith was leading the field in his No. 47 Boomershine Pontiac by more than 8 laps. However, misfortune struck when a piece of asphalt punctured his race car's gas tank and he ended up finishing in 12th place, 48 laps back.

38. The gas trucks ran out of gas at the halfway point of the 1962 Gwyn Staley 400 at the North Wilkesboro Speedway in North Carolina on April 15. In order to get gas for their race cars, pit crews ran through the infield with buckets and hoses, siphoning gas from passenger cars. A caution was thrown to allow a gas truck to leave in search of more gas, but the truck never returned.

39. Junior Johnson drove a No. 27 Ford in the 1965 Daytona 500. He had competed with the No. 27 painted on his cars for several years, however, while leading that race, his right front tire blew and he hit the wall on lap 27. Johnson was not injured, but he immediately changed to No. 26 from that point on.

40. On May 18, 1952, Ted Chamberlain carefully guided his speed-ing race car the final 120 laps of the 200-lap race at Dayton Speedway in Ohio with nothing more than a steering hub after the steering wheel fell off. He finished 13th out of 15 cars.

41. Former NASCAR premier series driver Janet Guthrie earned her pilot's license at age 17 and was able to fly more than 20 types of aircraft. She graduated from the University of Michigan with a degree in physics and worked as an aviation engineer and qualified for the NASA astronaut program. She was later disqualified from becoming an astronaut when NASA made having a Ph.D. a requirement.

42. Darlington Raceway in South Carolina got its egg shape when, during the construction, the land owner made one stipulation: that they not disturb his minnow pond, which sat on the track's property. That's why turns 3 and 4 are shorter than turns 1 and 2.

43. The finish to the 1993 Daytona 500 is considered one of the most memorable broadcast calls in NASCAR history. Ned Jarrett called the last half-lap of the race by himself as his partners in the booth gave way to his emotionally charged play-by-play. On the track, his son, Dale Jarrett, was fighting Dale Earnhardt for the victory in a tightly contested race. He let everyone listening know that the father-son tie is much stronger than any unbiased call he could've proffered: "Come on Dale, go baby go! All right! It's the Dale and Dale show, and you know who I'm pulling for!"

44. On October 23, 1994, Dale Earnhardt won the NASCAR premier series race at Rockingham Speedway in North Carolina, clinching the series championship with two races left to run in the season. The 1994 NASCAR championship was Earnhardt's 7th, tying him with Richard Petty for the most number of career titles in the series. He went on to finish 40th and 2nd in the final two races of the season.

45. In the inaugural Daytona 500 on February 22, 1959, Paul Bass drove an Edsel convertible to a 46th-place finish, out of 59 entrants. He only completed 52 of the scheduled 200 laps. It was the only appearance in a race by an Edsel in NASCAR history.

46. Of the 43 cars that started the June 13, 1954, race at Linden Airport, almost half of the cars (21) were foreign makes. This was the first time in NASCAR history that this many foreign cars raced in a NASCAR premier series race. There were 13 Jaguars, 5 Morris Garage, 1 Porsche, 1 Morgan and 1 Austin-Healy. Al Keller won the 50-lap event, leading 28 of them, driving a Jaguar — the first time a foreign make won a NASCAR premier series race.

47. Buck Baker won the May 20, 1956, NASCAR premier series race at Martinsville Speedway and Jack Smith won the October 28, 1956, NASCAR premier series event at Martinsville Speedway, while both driving the No. 502 Carl Kiekhaefer–owned Dodge. It is the highest–numbered race car to win any race in NASCAR's three national series. Smith also drove three races in the 1956 season piloting the No. 999 Ford owned by Joe Jones, but he didn't win any races.

48. *Forbes* magazine ranks the Daytona 500 as the world's seventh most valuable sporting event brand and the second-most valuable single telecast sporting event, trailing only the Super Bowl. The Daytona 500 ranks ahead of the NCAA Men's Final Four, MLB All-Star Week and the Kentucky Derby.

49. In order to promote the November 11, 1951, race in Gardena, California, at Carrell Speedway, NASCAR star Fonty Flock made appearances throughout southern California in his racing uniform, which consisted of a white button-down shirt, Bermuda shorts, knee socks and nice shoes.

50. Richard Petty supposedly won his first race in the NASCAR premier series at Lakewood Speedway in Atlanta, Georgia, on June 14, 1959. However, the driver who had finished in second place protested the win. After checking the scorecards, it was determined that Petty, indeed, did not win the race. The pro-tester was Lee Petty, Richard Petty's father, who ended up with the victory.

51. GRAND-AM Road Racing was established in 1999 to return stability to major league sports car road racing in North America. It began competition with the 2000 running of the Rolex 24 At Daytona. GRAND-AM was acquired by NASCAR Holdings in late 2008 and now operates as one organization.

52. Rusty Wallace is an avid aviator who owns several airplanes and a helicopter.

53. Davey Allison's first job was sweeping floors at his father's auto shop, Bobby Allison Racing, in Hueytown, Alabama.

54. Tiny Lund scored one of the most dramatic victories in NASCAR history in the 1963 Daytona 500. During practice for a sports car event at Daytona, Lund helped rescue driver Marvin Panch from a burning car. Lund replaced Panch in the Wood Brothers Ford and went on to win the race. He was awarded the Carnegie Medal for Heroism for saving Panch.

55. Prior to racing in the NASCAR premier series, Wendell Scott had been an army mechanic in World War II as well as a cab driver. When he returned from the war he opened a garage and worked on cars while racing, primarily on Virginia tracks.

56. On December 2, 2011, 83-year-old Robert Weaver was named the inaugural recipient of the Betty Jane France Humanitarian Award. Weaver delivers treats to deaf, blind and multi-disabled students and is lovingly referred to many in the Talladega area as the "Ice Cream Man." Among other prizes that Weaver received was $100,000 to be given to the charity of his choice, which was the Alabama Institute for Deaf and Blind.

57. NASCAR Unites is an industry-wide initiative, led by The NASCAR Foundation, that creates an opportunity for NASCAR fans, drivers, teams, tracks, sponsors and more to unite to improve the lives of children across the nation. NASCAR Unites engages the sport in a collaborative effort to support children's causes through volunteering, fundraising and sharing inspirational stories.

58. On August 21, 2010, Kyle Busch completed a sweep that had never been accomplished before in NASCAR history when he won all three national series races at the same race track in the same weekend. On August 18, 2010, Busch led 116 of 206 laps to win in the O'Reilly 200 at Bristol Motor Speedway in the NASCAR Camping World Truck Series. Two days later he won the Food City 250 on the same track, leading 116 of 250 laps. The next day, on August 21, 2010, Busch led 283 of 500 laps to earn his third trip to Victory Lane at Bristol that weekend.

59. On August 6, 1971, Bobby Allison led 138 of 250 laps in the race held at Bowman Gray Stadium in Winston-Salem, North Carolina. Although Allison crossed the finish line three seconds before second-place finisher Richard Petty, NASCAR did not officially count the victory toward Allison's career wins in the NASCAR premier series. Allison's car was a Grand American race car and not the style of cars they were running in the NASCAR Grand National Division (now the NASCAR Sprint Cup

Series) at the time. As a result, no driver is listed as the official winner of the race.

60. On June 6, 2009, after winning the NASCAR Nationwide Series event at Nashville Superspeedway, Kyle Busch did something unprecedented with his race trophy: he smashed it to pieces while still in Victory Lane. The trophy, in this instance, was a Sam Bass–painted Gibson Les Paul guitar.

61. On August 10, 2011, NASCAR announced that, for the 2012 NASCAR Sprint Cup Series season, Pocono Raceway's two events would be shortened from 500 to 400 miles. It would be the first time the triangular track would host a 400-mile event in the NASCAR premier series. Pocono started hosting NASCAR premier series races in 1974, hosting a single 500-mile event each year until 1982 when the track was given a second race. The track hosted two 500-mile events every year between 1982 and 2011.

62. At the beginning of 2011, NASCAR and teams throughout NASCAR's three national series pooled their intellectual properties for apparel, die-cast, toys and trackside distribution to create the NASCAR Team Properties. The model provides a more streamlined process for licensees and was designed to be more beneficial to teams, licensees, retailers, NASCAR and the fans. In June 2011, the NASCAR Team Properties was named the Best Sports Program of the Year by the International Licensing Industry and Merchandisers' Association.

63. In 2004, NASCAR launched the NASCAR Library Collection as part of their overall licensing operation, providing a level of authentication and quality to NASCAR-licensed books. The collection's motto is "Unbelievable Stories. Believable Source."

64. Indianapolis Motor Speedway was built in 1909 as a testing ground for the American automobile industry. The track was originally paved with crushed stones and then repaved with bricks, thus the track's nickname "The Brickyard." In 1961, the bricks were then covered with asphalt, leaving one yard of bricks at the start-finish line. The winner of the NASCAR Sprint Cup Series race, the Brickyard 400, receives a trophy with a brick atop a base. It is tradition for the winning team to line up and kiss the yard of bricks.

65. The 2011 NASCAR Sprint Cup Series season featured five first-time race winners in the series. Trevor Bayne kicked off the season with a surprising victory in the Daytona 500 in only his second career start in the series. A couple months later Regan Smith visited Victory Lane at Darlington Raceway. Then on July 2, David Ragan earned his first career win in the series at Daytona International Speedway. Later that month, Paul

Menard, alongside his father, kissed the "yard of bricks" at Indianapolis Motor Speedway. Two races later, Marcos Ambrose crossed the finish line first at Watkins Glen International.

66. In 1998, to celebrate its 50th anniversary, NASCAR listed the top 50 drivers in NASCAR history. Among the notables were future NASCAR Hall of Fame members Bobby Allison, Buck Baker, Dale Earnhardt, Richie Evans, Ned Jarrett, Junior Johnson, Cotton Owens, David Pearson, Lee Petty, Richard Petty, Herb Thomas, Rusty Wallace, Darrell Waltrip, Glen Wood and Cale Yarborough. Current drivers named to the list were Geoff Bodine, Bill Elliott, Jeff Gordon, Terry Labonte and Mark Martin.

67. In April 2009, NASCAR and iRacing announced a partnership to develop a NASCAR-sanctioned online racing series. The system allows fans from all over the world to compete head-to-head on virtual replicas of NASCAR-sanctioned tracks in cars that mirror the race cars the NASCAR teams develop. Even current NASCAR stars such as Dale Earnhardt Jr. and Brad Keselowski compete in iRacing competition.

68. The restrictor plate was re-introduced to NASCAR (after first being introduced on August 8, 1970) to slow down the speeds on some of the NASCAR-sanctioned tracks in 1988 after Bill Elliott posted a 212.809-mph qualifying speed for the May 1987 race at Talladega Superspeedway. Earlier that season, Elliott won the pole at the 1987 Daytona 500 with a qualifying speed of 210.364 mph. The 1988 Daytona 500 was the first race to have cars running with restrictor plates since their re-introduction. Bobby Allison won that first restrictor-plate race leading 70 of the 200 laps.

69. During a 2010 preseason press conference, NASCAR's Vice President of Competition Robin Pemberton stated "boys, have it at" in an attempt to lighten the reins on NASCAR drivers and allow the drivers to "self-police" themselves on track. As a result, the racing on track has been more action-packed than ever, with drivers not having to worry about being penalized as often in the past.

70. As of the beginning of the 2012 NASCAR Sprint Cup Series season, Wood Brothers Racing had won 98 races in the series, with at least one victory in each of the last seven decades. The team's first victory came at the hands of Glen Wood, one of the team's founders, when he led all 200 laps of the April 1960 race at Bowman Gray Stadium in Winston-Salem, North Carolina. Trevor Bayne scored the team's 98th victory in the 2011 Daytona 500 at Daytona International Speedway on February 20.

71. The 1974 Daytona 500 was actually the "Daytona 450" because NASCAR cut the distance of all their NASCAR premier series races by 10 percent in the first part of the season because of

America's energy crisis, which resulted in a reduction of 20 circuits around the track. Richard Petty led 73 of the 180 laps to win the Great American Race.

72. The 1967 Daytona 500 was the only NASCAR premier series victory for racing superstar Mario Andretti.

73. In November 2011, five current NASCAR Sprint Cup Series drivers had one of their children compete against three wild-card drivers selected from the crowd at Homestead-Miami Speedway in the first ever *NASCAR Unleashed* "Battle of the NASCAR Kids" hosted by the game's publisher, Activision. Each of the drivers' children participating were competing for a charity. In the end, Ryan Blaney, Dave Blaney's son, won $5,000 for the Alzheimer's Association.

74. In 1989, Darrell Waltrip finally won the Daytona 500 after leading 25 of the 200 laps. It was his 17th attempt. He was driving the No. 17 Tide Chevrolet owned by Hendrick Motorsports and pitted in pit stall No. 17.

75. Seven NASCAR premier series drivers have scored their first series win in the Daytona 500. They are Tiny Lund (1963), Mario Andretti (1967), Pete Hamilton (1970), Derrike Cope (1990), Sterling Marlin (1994), Michael Waltrip (2001) and Trevor Bayne (2011).

76. Upon seeing Daytona International Speedway for the first time prior to the 1959 Daytona 500, NASCAR premier series driver Jimmy Thompson said, "There have been other tracks that separated the men from the boys. This is the track that will separate the brave from the weak after the boys are gone."

77. Curtis Turner turned a speed of 180.831 mph during qualifying at the 1967 Daytona 500. It was the first time a NASCAR stock car had posted a qualifying speed over 180 mph.

78. Loy Allen Jr. (1994), Mike Skinner (1997) and Jimmie Johnson (2002) all won the pole for the Daytona 500 in their rookie seasons.

79. Race car drivers John Kennedy and George Bush both competed in the NASCAR premier series. Kennedy appeared in 8 races during the 1969 season and 11 races between 1977 and 1979. His best finish was at Atlanta Motor Speedway, where he placed 14th on August 10, 1969. Bush competed in 5 races in 1952 with a best finish of 7th at Lakewood Speedway in Georgia on November 16.

80. During the October 1976 race at Charlotte Motor Speedway, crew chief Leonard Wood radioed his driver David Pearson to warn him that the yellow flag was out. Pearson, who was spinning through the second turn after hooking bumpers with a slower car, calmly replied, "Yeah, I know. It's me."

81. The Coca-Cola 600, held each year over Memorial Day weekend at Charlotte Motor Speedway, has traditionally been the longest race held in NASCAR competition. However, Michigan International Speedway attempted to host a 600-mile event in August 1969. The race was called because of rain after 165 laps, short of the scheduled 300 laps. It was the only time a track has tried to stage a NASCAR-sanctioned 600-mile race outside of Charlotte.

82. Different tracks require tires with different make ups. Tires that go on the left side of a race car are considerably softer than right-side tires. It's against NASCAR's rules for a team to place tires meant for the left side of a race car on the right side and vice-versa.

83. Dale Earnhardt is the only driver in NASCAR premier series history to win the Rookie of the Year Award one year and then win the series championship the very next year. In 1979, Earnhardt's rookie season, he won one race and had 11 top-5 finishes, finishing in seventh place in the final points standings. The next year, Earnhardt won five races and scored 19 top-5 finishes, winning his first of seven NASCAR premier series championships beating runner up Cale Yarborough by 19 points.

84. NASCAR driver Frank Mundy hitched a ride about 2,000 miles to the April 8, 1951, NASCAR premier series race at Carrell Speedway in Gardena, California, with fellow driver Marshall Teague, who ended up winning the 200-lap event. Mundy didn't have a race car to compete in, but hoped to find one once he got out west. Unfortunately, he was unsuccessful in his attempts, so he rented a Chevrolet from a local car rental company and went on to finish 11th among the 20 race entrants. He returned the car to the rental company after hours so they would not see the badly worn tires on the car.

85. On November 15, 1992, in the NASCAR premier series season finale at Atlanta Motor Speedway, Alan Kulwicki led one more lap than the race-winner Bill Elliott earning him a 5-point bonus and clinching the series championship by a mere 10 points over Elliott. It was also the last race in Richard Petty's storied career and the first in the career of a promising young driver named Jeff Gordon.

86. The first NASCAR premier series race held under lights took place at Columbia Speedway (South Carolina) on June 16, 1951. Frank Mundy led 167 of the 200 laps on the half-mile track to win the event.

87. Darlington Raceway held two NASCAR premier series events in the same year for the first time in 1952. A 100-mile spring race run on May 10 was scheduled as a support event for NASCAR's new open-wheeled Speedway Division.

88. In August 1952, Cannonball Baker announced that any driver convicted of reckless driving on the highway would be regarded as violating the NASCAR rule book. He cited the fact that the NASCAR Grand National Division (now the NASCAR Sprint Cup Series) was in the public eye and drivers were expected to maintain a high level of dignity in their behavior off the track.

89. Legendary mechanic Smokey Yunick made his only NASCAR premier series start as a driver at Palm Beach Speedway in West Palm Beach, Florida, on November 30, 1952. Yunick qualified last in a 19-car field and finished 18th after completing only seven laps because of ignition problems.

90. The 2011 NASCAR Sprint Cup Series season was the most competitive season, in regard to statistics, in the history of the series. Races averaged 27.1 lead changes (most in the history of the series), 12.8 leaders (the highest average since 1949) and there were 131,989 green-flag passes during the entire season (which is the highest number of green-flag passes since NASCAR started keeping record of the stat in 2005).

91. Glenn "Fireball" Roberts won his first intermediate-track race on July 4, 1956, at Raleigh Speedway in North Carolina. The win was protested by Carl Kiekhaefer, the owner of Speedy Thompson's second-place car, on the grounds that Kiekhaefer thought Robert's car carried an underweight flywheel. The track did not have a scale for such a situation, so the flywheel was weighed at a nearby fish market. NASCAR determined the weight of the flywheel was within their rules and the win stood.

92. The only person injured as a result of a wreck at the July 9, 1961, NASCAR premier series event at Atlanta Motor Speedway was wrecker driver Robert Higgenbottom, whose vehicle flipped over while he was retrieving a crashed race car.

93. NASCAR star Junior Johnson attempted to qualify for the 1963 Indianapolis 500 at Indianapolis Motor Speedway. The traditional roadster he drove was unusual in that it sported a complete roll cage, the only Indy car to do so.

94. Four-time Indianapolis 500 winner Johnny Rutherford made his NASCAR debut in a 1963 Daytona 500 qualifying race, which he won after leading 6 of the 40 laps. Two days later he would finish the Great American Race in 9th place, 4 laps back of the race winner Tiny Lund.

95. Cale Yarborough temporarily left NASCAR to drive Indy cars during the 1971 and 1972 seasons. During his "absence" from

NASCAR, Yarborough competed in nine races in the NASCAR premier series with one top-5 finish.

96. Talladega Superspeedway in Alabama hosted its first NASCAR premier series race on September 14, 1969. Richard Brickhouse led 33 of the 188 laps in the 500-mile event on his way to Victory Lane. It was his first and only victory in the series.

97. Action sports star Travis Pastrana was set to make his NASCAR debut in a July 2011 NASCAR Nationwide Series event. However, shortly before the race, Pastrana broke his right ankle during the X Games, delaying his debut in NASCAR. He is expected to attempt his NASCAR debut again during the 2012 season.

98. On September 30, 1970, the NASCAR premier series hosted its final dirt-track race with Richard Petty taking the checkered flag at the North Carolina State Fairgrounds in Raleigh.

99. In January 2003, NASCAR unveiled the 61,000-square foot NASCAR Research and Development Center in Concord, North Carolina. The research and work done at the facility is focused on improving safety initiatives, enhancing competition and cutting costs for NASCAR teams.

100. Dick Hagey of Philadelphia, Pennsylvania, appeared in one NASCAR premier series race. On June 21, 1953, Hagey drove a

Volkswagen Beetle in the June 21, 1953, race at Langhorne Speedway where he finished 19th in a 38-car field, after qualifying 32nd. It is the only race in the series in which a Volkswagen Beetle competed.

101. On February 25, 1956, Pete Peterson, an auto air-conditioner salesman from Chicago, entered a 1956 Ford convertible in the first NASCAR Convertible Division race, which was held on the Daytona Beach & Road Course. With the convertible top and windows up, Peterson qualified 28th out of 28 drivers and finished the race in 10th place. After the race, Peterson said the temperature inside the car was comfortable and predicted that air-conditioned race cars would soon replace the non-air-conditioned cars.

102. On May 2, 1959, Junior Johnson flipped his car during practice at Hickory Motor Speedway in North Carolina. Not willing to give up, Johnson banged out the dents in the race car in time for the race and ended up leading 38 of the 250 laps to take the win.

103. For the 1957 NASCAR premier series season, Ford offered a supercharger on its 312-cubic-inch engine while GM and Chevrolet added a fuel injection system to its 283-cubic-inch engine. Both options were legal according to NASCAR rules at the time. However, by the end of April 1957, Bill France banned these options afraid that the horsepower and speed would get out of hand. Teams running Fords and Chevrolets had to use conventional carburetion for the rest of the season.

104. On April 1, 1962, Herman "The Turtle" Beam drew the pole position for the NASCAR premier series race at Richmond International Raceway after qualifying was rained out. On the pace lap, Beam pulled onto pit road to allow the entire field to pass him. After coming in 12th place out of 25 drivers, Beam explained that he was not comfortable starting in front of all the "hot dogs."

105. After the August 4, 1963, NASCAR premier series race at Nashville Speedway, Cale Yarborough got yelled at by Herman Beam, his car owner, for – of all things – going too fast. Beam felt that Yarborough was being too rough on his Ford. During the race, in which he placed eighth, Yarborough was bumped by another car leaving a dent in the door. After the race Beam told Yarborough, "You see there? If you would've slowed down he'd missed you!"

106. The No. 13 was a major superstition for race car drivers for decades. Among the most superstitious drivers was Joe Weatherly. The 1962 Southern 500 at Darlington Raceway would have been the 13th running of the event, but Weatherly, who was a popular driver and a good draw to pull fans to the race, told the track's president Bob Colvin that he refused to race in the event because it was being called the 13th running of the event. To placate Weatherly, Colvin renamed the 1962 Southern 500 the "12th Renewal Southern 500."

107. Curtis Turner and Bobby Isaac were involved in a heated battle during the September 26, 1965, NASCAR premier series race at Martinsville Speedway. Isaac bumped Turner knocking both cars into the wall and out of the race. Turner jumped from his car and ran to Isaac yelling "I want to know if you wrecked me on purpose?" Isaac replied, "No, I didn't wreck you on purpose. Why would I do that? I don't even know you."

108. After winning the March 27, 1966, NASCAR premier series race at Atlanta Motor Speedway, Jim Hurtubise confessed to using a device that lowered his car during the race. "I carried a big monkey wrench with me. On caution laps I'd crank a bolt and lower the body so it would cut the air better. After the race was over, I drove real slow on the backstretch. I slung the wrench into the infield. I didn't want anybody to see that wrench in the car when I got to Victory Lane. They might have suspected something."

109. Curtis Turner drove in style for the August 18, 1966, NASCAR premier series race at Columbia Speedway (South Carolina) when he drove his Junior Johnson–owned Ford to a third-place finish while wearing a three-piece business suit. Turner had the following to say about his race uniform that day, "Johnson's sponsor, Holly Farms Poultry, told me that if I was gonna drive for them, I would have to wear a suit. They wanted me to be a gentleman driver and I figured this was the first step. You've gotta look good, you know."

110. The iconic winged cars from Chrysler – the Dodge Daytona and Plymouth Superbird – were intended to be run on speedways a mile long or longer. The Superbird never competed on a NASCAR short track, but the Dodge Daytona appeared on short tracks twice during the 1970 NASCAR premier series season. Buddy Baker drove the Neil Castles–owned Dodge Daytona at International Raceway Park in Ona, West Virginia, on August 11 to a 21st-place finish after experiencing brake problems. On October 18, Dave Marcis finished in 25th place in a Daytona at Martinsville Speedway after quitting the event in solidarity with a dozen other independent racers in a protest over prize-money distribution.

111. On April 8, 1971, Neil Castles named the Dodge he drove in the race at Columbia Speedway the "Free Lt. Calley Special" after Lt. William Calley, who was in the news for his part in the My Lai Massacre in Vietnam.

112. When Bobby Isaac won the NASCAR premier series event at

Greenville-Pickens Speedway (South Carolina) on April 10, 1971, it was the first time a NASCAR event was televised live, flag-to-flag. ABC Sports broadcast the event.

113. The July 1998 NASCAR premier series event at Daytona International Speedway was postponed to October 1998 after wild fires ravaged the Daytona Beach area for several weeks during the summer. The October race was the first race run under the world's largest lighting system.

114. Grand Prix and Indianapolis 500 champion Jimmy Clark made only one start in the NASCAR premier series. Clark qualified 24th for the October 29, 1967, race at Rockingham Speedway. His "relief driver" was fellow Grand Prix driver Jochen Rindt. After qualifying his Holman Moody–owned Ford, Clark called his girlfriend in Europe to tell her, "You won't believe it, love. They have me climbing in through the bloody window." Clark's No. 66 Ford fell out of the race after only 144 laps (finishing 30th out of 44), before Rindt had a chance to replace him.

115. Open-wheel racer Tony Bonadies made NASCAR history when his car's owner, Red Crise, brought an old army-type walkie-talkie to Darlington Raceway in 1952 so he could communicate with his pit crew during the 1952 NASCAR Speedway Division season. The huge walkie-talkie was attached to Bonadies' leather-strapped helmet. Bonadies had to press the talk button to communicate with his team in an exercise Crise deemed successful despite static and engine noise. During the race, the car blew a head gasket ending their day and leaving Crise with a blown engine and Bonadies with a headache.

116. Inaugural NASCAR Hall of Fame member Junior Johnson, who was infamous for his moonshine-running past and even spent time in prison for making the illegal drink, donated a working moonshine still to be displayed at the NASCAR Hall of Fame in uptown Charlotte, North Carolina, when it opened in 2010. Johnson even drove a couple hours from his home to help the NASCAR Hall of Fame staff construct the still for display after they initially struggled to piece all the parts together.

117. Glenn Dunaway of Gastonia, North Carolina, was initially credited with the win at the first NASCAR premier series race on June 19, 1949, at Charlotte Fairgrounds Speedway (North Carolina). However, Dunaway was stripped of the distinction after it was discovered that his car had illegal rear springs. The unprecedented decision to take the win away from Dunaway was even upheld in court.

118. On October 5, 2010, Englishman Richard Towler was crowned the inaugural champion of the NASCAR iRacing.com Series. For winning the NASCAR-sanctioned series, Towler was a guest of honor at the 2010 Ford Championship Weekend at Homestead-Miami Speedway where he accepted a $10,000 check during pre-race festivities.

119. From 1952 to 1954, NASCAR sanctioned the NASCAR Hawaiian Division that raced solely on tracks in Hawaii. This was prior to Hawaii becoming a state, which happened in 1959. The drivers mainly raced in modified pre-war coupes. One of the venues that held races was the Honolulu Stadium.

120. The Hudson Hornet only appeared in NASCAR premier series competition from 1951 until partway through the 1955 season. In that small span of time, drivers of the Hudson Hornet racked up an amazing 79 wins, the last of which was a Herb Thomas win on February 6, 1955 at Palm Beach Speedway (Florida). Thomas drove the car to two series championships in 1951 and 1953, while Tim Flock drove a Hudson Hornet to the 1952 championship. Other race winners in the Hudson were Buck Baker, Bob Flock, Fonty Flock, Al Keller, Hershel McGriff, Dick Rathmann, Buddy Shuman, Marshall Teague and Donald Thomas.

121. In 2002, NASCAR became the world's first major auto racing sanctioning body to mandate the use of an approved head and neck restraint by all drivers on every type of race circuit.

122. After seven years of research and development out of the NASCAR R&D Center, NASCAR debuted a new car in the NASCAR Sprint Cup Series in 2007. The car was developed to improve driver safety, cut costs and offer better on-track competition.

123. On April 4, 2008, Michael McDowell hit the outside wall hard and flipped his car eight times in a qualifying run at Texas Motor Speedway. As a result of the NASCAR R&D's work to make the race cars safer, McDowell walked away from the wreck without any injuries.

124. Years ago, race coverage was often not nationwide and it wasn't clearly defined which channel would air that week's race, making it hard for fans to find the events. In 2001, NASCAR negotiated a TV contract with FOX, FX, NBC and TNT to carry the three national touring series. Then in 2007, NASCAR entered into a new deal with ABC, ESPN, FOX, SPEED and TNT to televise the races.

125. On April 16, 2011, Jeff Gordon posted the slowest winning pole speed at Talladega Superspeedway in the track's NASCAR Sprint Cup Series history with a speed of 178.248 mph.

126. Shortly after retiring from driving in NASCAR in 1992, Richard Petty was awarded the Presidential Medal of Freedom – which is the United States' highest civilian award – by President George H.W. Bush. Petty is the only person in motorsports to receive this prestigious award.

127. The February 18, 1979, Daytona 500 was one of the most memorable races in NASCAR history and helped boost NASCAR's popularity. On the last lap of the famous race, Donnie Allison and Cale Yarborough were fighting for the lead when their cars made contact with each other and the turn-3 wall. They ended up in the infield grass as Richard Petty sped past on his way to victory closely followed by Darrell Waltrip and A.J. Foyt. However, Petty's victory was quickly overshadowed by what was happening in the infield grass. Yarborough and Allison, along with his older brother Bobby, had got out of their race cars to brawl, while the cameras continued to roll and televise the fight nationally. The race drew huge ratings, partly due to the large snowstorm that had hit most of the east coast.

128. On February 14, 1988, Bobby Allison, in the No. 12 Miller High Life Buick, celebrated his third and final Daytona 500 in Victory Lane with his son, Davey, after leading 70 of the 200 laps. Davey joined his father after finishing second and leading two laps in the Great American Race, piloting the No. 28 Havoline Ford. Bobby would end up retiring from racing four months later. A few years later, Davey would claim his own Daytona 500 victory winning the 1992 race.

129. After an all-night drive from upstate New York to a July 4, 1953, NASCAR premier series event at Piedmont Interstate Fairgrounds in Spartanburg, South Carolina, drivers Herb Thomas and Tim Flock decided to take a nap in the infield grass of the race track. During the early morning a Champion Spark Plug rep ran over the drivers with his passenger car while putting up banners. Thomas was unhurt, but the car parked on Flock's head, inflicting injuries that kept him from competing for several weeks. Flock's injuries were lessened because of a rainstorm a few days earlier that softened the ground.

130. Lee Petty was racing at McCormick Field in Asheville, North Carolina, on July 12, 1958, when, during one of the preliminary races, his Oldsmobile was bumped by Cotton Owens driving a Pontiac. The impact sent Petty off the race track and into one of the baseball dugouts.

131. Tiny Lund flipped his Chevrolet during the October 9, 1955, NASCAR premier series race at Memphis-Arkansas Speedway in LeHi, Arkansas. His seat belt broke and he was tossed from the car. He survived, but in an ironic twist, his sponsor that day was Rupert Seat Belts.

132. In August 1961, Curtis Turner and Tim Flock were banned for life from NASCAR competition. The two drivers attempted to unionize the other drivers through the controversial Teamsters

Union. Flock retired from racing while Turner returned to NASCAR in 1965.

133. During a race at Lakewood Speedway in Atlanta, Wilbur Rakestraw went off the third turn into what he thought was a lake that took up most of the infield. Rakestraw soon learned that the lake was actually a cesspool. Thanks to his training as a Navy Seal, he survived the incident, although no one would go near him once he returned to pit road.

134. The media covering the 1966 Southern 500 at Darlington Raceway (South Carolina) revolted against the track's conditions after Earl Balmer nearly knocked down the press box during the race. The press members presented the track president Bob Colvin with a petition. The petition read, "We the undersigned do hereby notify Darlington Raceway that we will not endanger our lives in the future covering Darlington events from the existing press location. We hereby request that the location of the press box be moved to a site affording better safety facilities and a better view of the race track. We are of the opinion that the present press box at the track is without equal in racing from the standpoint of peril to human life. And we refuse the responsibility for this condition in order to serve the Raceway."

135. A full-fledged moonshine still was found under Middle Georgia

Raceway in Macon in November 1967. An entrance, with a 35-foot ladder leading to a 125-foot tunnel, was found under a ticket booth. The still could produce 200 gallons every five days. The operation included a 2,000-gallon cooker, a 1,200-gallon box fermenter and a 750-gallon gas tank for cooking. The track operator was charged with possession of apparatus for the distillery of illegal liquor, but was later found not guilty.

136. On April 12, 1970, a fan at Talladega Superspeedway threw a glass bottle over the fence onto the track. The bottle hit the windshield of Cale Yarborough's Mercury, shattering the glass. Although Yarborough continued the race without a windshield, glass bottles have been banned at all NASCAR races since that day.

137. After David Pearson hit the inside wall at Bristol Motor Speedway on July 19, 1970, Pearson had this to say about the wreck. "That was a hard lick. I've always been told that if you hit something hard enough to knock your shoes off, you're dead. When I came to, I looked on the floorboard and saw my shoes laying there I thought for sure I was dead."

138. Two NASCAR premier series events have been postponed because of snow conditions. The most recent was the March 20, 1993, race at Atlanta Motor Speedway.

139. An overanxious Cale Yarborough, running third at Richmond International Raceway on March 7, 1976, brushed the outside wall, sending him into the inside wall and a parked fire truck. No one was injured, but an embarrassed Yarborough claimed that he just lost control while trying too hard to catch Richard Petty.

140. Canadian Earl Ross, Italian Mario Andretti, Colombian Juan Pablo Montoya and Australian Marcos Ambrose are the only four foreign-born drivers to win a NASCAR premier series event.

141. On January 24, 2012, Ford revealed the street and race car versions of their 2013 Ford Fusion. The race car will hit the NASCAR Sprint Cup Series tracks in 2013. To answer fans' concerns about the differences in appearance between the street and race car versions the stock cars that will be seen on race tracks in 2013 will look very similar to the cars that fans can purchase at dealerships.

142. On November 20, 2011, Tony Stewart won the NASCAR Sprint Cup Series championship with crew chief Darian Grubb making some crucial calls down the stretch to help Stewart capture his third series championship. However, the day after winning the title, Grubb was released by Stewart-Haas Racing. A couple weeks later he landed at Joe Gibbs Racing as the crew chief for the No. 11 FedEx Chevrolet driven by Denny Hamlin.

143. As of the end of the 2011 NASCAR Nationwide Series season, there are seven drivers who have won two championships in the series: Jack Ingram (1982, 1985); Sam Ard (1983, 1984); Larry Pearson (1986, 1987); Randy LaJoie (1996, 1997); Dale Earnhardt Jr. (1998, 1999); Kevin Harvick (2001, 2006) and Martin Truex Jr. (2004, 2005).

144. Longstanding NASCAR licencee Press Pass, founded in 1992, staked its claim as a revolutionary trendsetter in the trading card industry by incorporating the first-ever athlete-worn or -used memorabilia into its trading cards. In its January 1996 Press Pass NASCAR trading cards, race-used tires were incorporated, and later that year they introduced race-used sheet metal cards and race-used Dale Ernhardt firesuit cards.

145. In 1950, Bill Rexford won the NASCAR premier series championship rather controversially. NASCAR penalized drivers Lee Petty and Red Byron with points deductions for running in non-NASCAR-sanctioned events, giving the title to Rexford.

146. In 2010, Chip Ganassi became the first owner in motorsports history to win three of the biggest American auto races in the same year – the Daytona 500, the Indianapolis 500 and the Brickyard 400.

147. Clint Bowyer is such a huge Elvis Presley fan that he considers meeting Elvis's daughter, Lisa Marie, during the race weekend at the Memphis Motorsports Park, one of the off-the-track highlights from his 2005 NASCAR Nationwide Series season.

148. Prior to the 2011 season, NASCAR changed the rules on qualifying for the Chase for the NASCAR Sprint Cup. At the end of the first 26 races, the top-10 drivers in the points standings automatically qualify for the Chase. The last two positions would be wild card spots awarded to the two drivers ranked between 11th and 20th with the most wins through the first 26 races. The drivers in the top 12 would then have their points reset with each Chase qualifier receiving 2,000 points. Each driver not in a wild card spot would receive 3 additional points for each race win up to the start of the Chase. The two wild card drivers' points would stay at 2,000, regardless of how many wins they had.

149. Most everyone knows that Richard Petty and Dale Earnhardt have won seven NASCAR premier series championships, but there are two other drivers who have won seven NASCAR championships. Steve Kosiski of Omaha, Nebraska, won seven championships in the O'Reilly Auto Parts All-Star Series, NASCAR Touring between 1987 and 1998. Jim Reed of Peekskill, New York, won five straight Short Track Division championships between 1953 and 1957 and two championships in the Eastern Late Model in 1960 and 1961. Richie Evans (NASCAR Modified Tour [9]) and Mike Stefanik (NASCAR Modified Tour [7]) and NASCAR K&N Pro Series [2]) have both won nine NASCAR championships.

150. Denny Hamlin started racing karts at age seven. His family believed so much that one day he would be a successful race car driver that they poured all they had into supporting Denny's motorsports career. His family struggled financially so he could pursue his dream, eventually proving the investment a sound one.

151. Through the 2011 NASCAR Sprint Cup Series season there have been 20 different winners in 80 Chase for the NASCAR Sprint Cup races: Greg Biffle, Clint Bowyer, Jeff Burton, Kurt Busch, Kyle Busch, Dale Earnhardt Jr., Carl Edwards, Jeff Gordon, Denny Hamlin, Kevin Harvick, Dale Jarrett, Jimmie Johnson, Kasey Kahne, Matt Kenseth, Mark Martin, Jamie McMurray, Joe Nemechek, Ryan Newman, Tony Stewart and Brian Vickers.

152. Bobby Labonte began his motorsports career in 1984, working as a crew member with Hagan Racing's No. 44 Chevrolet driven by his brother, Terry Labonte.

153. NASCAR Sprint Cup Series drivers and brothers Terry and Bobby Labonte were inducted into the Texas Sports Hall of Fame in 2001, the fifth and sixth race car drivers to receive such distinction. Included in their class were Troy Aikman, Dick "Night Train" Lane, Bruce Matthews, Mike Munchak and Norm Cash.

154. Mark Martin has received many honors and distinctions throughout his career from various outlets. In 2009, Martin was recognized as *NASCAR Illustrated*'s "Person of the Year Presented by Old Spice." He has also earned the *Sporting News'* Dale Earnhardt Tough Driver Award, was named to the All-America Team selected by the American Auto Racing Writers & Broadcasters Association (AARWBA) and was crowned the Sportsman of the Year by the *Arkansas Democrat-Gazette* in his home state. Additionally, he was nominated for the SPEED Performer of the Year.

155. In 2002, Jeff Gordon and Juan Pablo Montoya, when he still drove Formula One, traded cars for a publicity event. Gordon drove Montoya's F1 car and Montoya drove Gordon's stock car.

156. Tony Stewart's favorite driver is four-time Indy 500 champion A.J. Foyt. Foyt drove the No. 14 in the IndyCar Series and is part of the reason Stewart selected the No. 14 for his new ride at Stewart-Haas Racing in 2009.

157. On Friday, May 24, 2002, Brian Vickers qualified 8th for the NASCAR Nationwide Series race at Charlotte Motor Speedway. After he was finished qualifying he drove back to his home in Trinity, North Carolina, for graduation ceremonies. He returned to Charlotte Motor Speedway on Saturday, May 25, 2002, in time for the start of the NASCAR Nationwide race where he finished 26th out of 43 entrants.

158. Dale Earnhardt appeared in the 1998 movie *BASEketball* starring Trey Parker and Matt Stone. Earnhardt played himself as a taxi driver. He also appeared as a NASCAR driver in the 1983 movie *Stroker Ace* starring Burt Reynolds. NASCAR drivers Neil Bonnett, Harry Gant, Terry Labonte, Benny Parsons, Kyle Petty, Tim Richmond, Ricky Rudd and Cale Yarborough also appeared in the flick.

159. In 2007, the pizza chain Domino's sponsored David Reutimann's No. oo Toyota for seven races in the NASCAR premier series because the pizza restaurant offered a deal where customers could buy one large pizza and get a second one of equal or lesser value for free – the two zeroes representing the two pizzas.

160. From 2006 through 2008, David Reutimann drove the Michael Waltrip–owned No. 99 race car sponsored by Aaron's in the NASCAR Nationwide Series because the retailer offered $99 rentals.

161. In eight races during the 1956 NASCAR premier series season and one race in the 1958 season, Bobby Johns of Miami, Florida, competed in the No. 7A Chevrolet that he owned. The "A" in the race car's number stood for his sister, Angeline.

162. In 1960, Roy Tyner of Red Springs, North Carolina, carried John F. Kennedy presidential nomination stickers on his race car while he competed.

163. In 1978, Jimmy Carter invited NASCAR drivers and owners to the White House. However, President Carter was unable to receive them as he was at Camp David negotiating a peace treaty.

164. Hollywood stunt driver Hal Needham and movie star Burt Reynolds were the original owners of the No. 33 Skoal Bandit race car piloted to victory nine times by Harry Gant between the 1981 and 1988 NASCAR premier series seasons.

165. *Thunder in Carolina*, which came out in 1960, was filmed during the 1959 Southern 500 and starred Rory Calhoun and Alan Hale Jr. NASCAR drivers with roles in the movie included Buck Baker, Joe Caspolich, Neil Castles, Joe Eubanks, Shep Langdon, Curtis Turner and Joe Weatherly.

166. In 1977, Richard Pryor portrayed Wendell Scott in *Greased Lightning*, which was based on the story of Scott's life.

167. The Red Bull Toyota that competed in the NASCAR Sprint Cup Series prior to the 2012 season, piloted mainly by Brian Vickers, carried the No. 83 because a can of Red Bull holds 8.3 ounces.

168. In 1966, John Jay Hooker was running for governor of Tennessee when he came up with a creative marketing campaign. He sponsored Buddy Baker's No. 00 car in the NASCAR premier series event on July 24 at Bristol Motor Speedway. The paint scheme incorporated the double zeroes as part of Hooker's last name.

169. Cale Yarborough was not the first race car driver to win three straight championships (1976–78). in a NASCAR-sanctioned series as many believe. From 1950 to 1952, Mike Klapak of Warren, Ohio, won the championship in the NASCAR Sportsman Division, the precursor to today's NASCAR Nationwide Series. Also beating Yarborough to the three straight NASCAR titles were Carl Stevens (1967–69, NASCAR Modified Tour), Ray Elder (1969–72, what is now the NASCAR K&N Pro Series West) and Jerry Cook (1974–77, NASCAR Modified Tour).

170. Lee Petty would not let his son, Richard, race in the NASCAR premier series until the latter's 21st birthday. Richard turned 21 on July 2, 1958, however, he didn't appear in a series race until July 18, 1958, at Canadian National Exhibition Speedway in Toronto, where he finished 17th out of 19 competitors after his father ran him into the wall.

171. The spoiler was first introduced to NASCAR competition by Sam McQuagg at the July 4, 1966, race at Daytona International Speedway. McQuagg was competing in a new Dodge Charger that had a very short deck lid that allowed air to get under the rear of the car causing it to lift off the track at high speeds. His owner, Ray Nichels, lobbied NASCAR to allow him to use the two-inch strip of metal across the deck lid. McQuagg led 126 of the 160 laps and beat Darel Dieringer to the finish line.

172. When car owner Junior Johnson showed up at the August 7, 1966, race at Atlanta Motor Speedway with his No. 26 Ford Galaxy, the yellow car didn't resemble the model that fans could purchase at car dealerships. The roof was lower, the front end had a steeper slope, the windshield was more reclined and the deck lid had more upward sweep than the street version of the same car. Fred Lorenzen qualified "the banana" third, and actually led 24 of the 267 laps before wrecking on lap 139, ending the race 23rd out of 42 drivers.

The oddly shaped car forced NASCAR officials to institute a new inspection policy using templates taken from stock vehicles.

173. On May 25, 1975, an estimated 90,600 fans were on hand at Charlotte Motor Speedway to witness the NASCAR premier series debut of a little-known driver by the name of Dale Earnhardt. Most fans in the stands just assumed Earnhardt was a local kid who probably had this one shot to make it in the series. Most fans knew of his father, Ralph Earnhardt, who was successful on the local short tracks, but never had much success on the superspeedways. Dale qualified 33rd in his Ed Negre–owned Dodge and finished 22nd out of 40 drivers. No one in the stands that day realized they were witnessing the series debut of one of the greatest drivers in NASCAR history. He only appeared in eight other races between 1975 and 1978.

174. On February 15, 1976, David Pearson and Richard Petty put on a show for the ages in the Daytona 500. Pearson and Petty dueled neck-and-neck, battling for the lead in the Great American Race. On the last lap of the race the two competitors approached the third turn and Petty moved into the lead. Their two cars touched and sent both into the wall. Petty's No. 43 STP Dodge slid into the infield. Pearson bounced his No. 21 Purolator Mercury off the No. 18 Chevrolet of Joe Frasson. Frasson headed down pit road while Petty and Pearson redirected their focus on getting to the finish line ahead of the other. Only Petty's race car wouldn't restart, while Pearson was able to keep his car running and soared across the finish line at a blistering speed of 20 mph. It is Pearson's only Daytona 500 victory, but years later fans and historians alike consider it the best finish in NASCAR history.

175. Although Jeff Gordon didn't make his NASCAR premier series debut until November 15, 1992, the NASCAR Nationwide Series race at Atlanta Motor Speedway on March 14, 1992, might be a more important date in the career of the young stock car driver. At the same track where Gordon would make his NASCAR premier series debut, the 21-year-old led the 43-car field for 103 of the 197 intervals around the track to win the NASCAR Nationwide Series race. Meanwhile, NASCAR premier series owner Rick Hendrick was watching the young driver closely and was impressed with what he saw. By year's end, Hendrick signed Gordon to a long-term deal to drive one of his race cars in the NASCAR premier series.

176. On April 2, 2000, the Petty family made history, but it wasn't "The King," Lee or Kyle to drive the family to the record book on this day. Instead, it was Adam Petty, Kyle's 19-year-old son, when he started in his first NASCAR premier series race at Texas Motor Speedway. Adam is not only the first fourth-generation driver to compete in a NASCAR premier series race, but he is the first fourth-generation athlete in the history of all professional sports. He started his only race in the series 33rd and finished 40th.

177. In the early 1980s, UNO sponsored the No. 1 race car owned by Hoss Ellington. Lake Speed competed in the card game-sponsored race car in 18 NASCAR premier series events in 1983. In 1982, Donnie Allison, Buddy Baker, Benny Parsons and Kyle Petty piloted the UNO-sponsored race car in a combined 21 races in the series. The previous year, Baker drove the vehicle in 15 races.

178. Rick Hendrick, 13-time championship owner in the three national series, has strapped himself in the pilot's seat of a NASCAR race car several times over his career. In both 1987 and 1988, Hendrick competed in a single race in the NASCAR premier series. In 1987, he started 21st at a race at Riverside International Raceway and finished 33rd after having transmission problems in a self-owned Chevrolet. The following year, Hendrick appeared in a race at the same race track and finished 15th after starting 13th. He has only competed in one race in the NASCAR Nationwide Series – at Road Atlanta Speedway, where he finished 24th after starting 6th. Hendrick also appeared in one race in the NASCAR Camping World Truck Series at Heartland Park Topeka in 1995 where he finished 23rd after starting 16th.

179. For three seasons (2006–08), Clint Bowyer drove the Richard Childress–owned No. 07 Chevrolet. During the time that Bowyer piloted the No. 07 race car, Jack Daniel's sponsored the car under their No. 7 brand of whiskey.

180. J.D. Gibbs, the son of current NASCAR owner Joe Gibbs, appeared in five NASCAR Nationwide Series races for Joe Gibbs Racing between the 1998 and 1999 seasons. He also appeared in one race for his father at Rockingham Speedway in 1999 in the NASCAR Camping World Truck Series.

181. Richard Petty holds the record for the longest consecutive streak of being in the top 10 in the points standings in the NASCAR premier series. He was in the top 10 in the points standings after 197 consecutive races, from February 24, 1967, to November 22, 1970. Bobby Allison is in second with 187 races, while Lee Petty (179), Dale Earnhardt (175) and Lee Petty (165) again round out the top five.

ACKNOWLEDGMENTS

I've always viewed acknowledgments in a book sort of like an acceptance speech a celebrity gives at a glitzy awards ceremony. Much like the limited time an actor is given to thank everyone, from a co-actor to a director to their parents and even sometimes a grade-school teacher, an author is given a very limited amount of words to thank and "acknowledge" everyone he can cram into a few hundred words before the red light flashes, warning him that he needs to wrap it up.

While I'm certainly no celebrity or actor, and I'm not onstage accepting an award in front of the masses, but instead sitting at my desk typing away, there are definitely plenty of people who I'd be remiss not to mention, either for their true assistance throughout the course of writing this trivia book or simply because they might lay a serious guilt trip on my conscience – one that I could certainly do without.

I must first give a big thank you to Jordan Fenn at Fenn/McClelland & Stewart for providing me this wonderful opportunity and the assistance he provided over our many conversations. In addition, I would like to thank Michael Melgaard for his editorial prowess and Andrew Roberts for assistance in designing a format that really works.

I'm indebted to Blake Davidson, Nick Rend and Nancy Czajkowski of NASCAR for allowing me to seize this opportunity when they could have just as easily said "no." I need to proffer a huge helping of gratitude to Buz McKim and Joelle Lapsley of the NASCAR Hall of Fame and Ken Martin with the NASCAR Media Group. Without their assistance and their willingness to allow me to pick their brains for entertaining stories, interesting facts and intriguing trivia, this book would have never got off the ground. Also, a huge thank you to Marty Smith of ESPN for taking time out of his busy, non-stop schedule to write the introduction.

Thanks Mom and Dad for being there whenever I needed you in the past, present and, I'm sure of it, the future. Additionally, I must also acknowledge the many family game nights growing up where Missy, Abby, Cindy and I all sat spellbound at dad's vast amount of trivia knowledge by way of *Trivial Pursuit*. In a way, I've picked up a bit of his love for trivia . . . no matter how trivial.

Finally, I would be absolutely mistaken if I didn't thank my wife, Renee, and my two sons, Hayden and Liam, for, among many other things, their encouragement, motivation and patience throughout my tireless pursuit of seeking out trivia and entertaining facts. Though it might sound a bit cliché here, if it wasn't for your and the boys' total understanding and support, this book would still be on my desktop waiting for me to dive in.

That red light that actors, musicians and directors receive when their time is up has flashed and I must exit stage right. I hope you come to look at this book as a resource for your NASCAR knowledge, and possibly even use it to stump or enlighten your friends. So, whether you're an avid NASCAR fan or someone just getting into the sport, I hope you learned something you didn't already know. Or, at the least, came across an interesting story, as NASCAR's history is chock full of colorful characters and stories.